Derrick Adams Prints

TANDEM PRESS

Derrick Adams: An Introduction

Katie Geha

Derrick Adams first visited Tandem Press in the spring of 2019, following the recommendation of his close friend Mickalene Thomas, who had recently completed a series of multi-process prints with the Press. Drawing from a previous painting, Adams worked with Tandem's Collaborative Printmakers, Jason Ruhl and Joe Freye, to create *Self Portrait on Float*, a striking image of the artist reclining on a unicorn-shaped pool float. His arms rest casually around the inflated creature, which is adorned with playful, opulent details: a gold-leaf chain, a gold tooth, and a rainbow-colored mane. Adams's figure fills the frame; he gazes out at the viewer with his head gently tilted, surrounded by a sea of brilliant teal. This print, along with some 20 others he would create with Tandem between 2019 and 2025, centers the leisure and lives of Black people. These images challenge historical narratives and offer vibrant affirmations of identity, presence, and everyday celebration.

Derrick Adams is known for his dynamic visual language, which spans collage, sculpture, installation, performance, and video. In his print collaborations with Tandem, he amplifies the formal intensity of his figures, prompting the printers to explore inventive techniques. For *Self Portrait on Float*, Adams and the team developed a 94-piece puzzle-cut woodblock, an ambitious technical feat that reflects the dedication to experimentation fundamental to his practice. In subsequent projects, Adams continued to expand his aesthetic vocabulary, this time through screen printing, working closely with Tandem's Collaborative Printer Patrick Smyczek to achieve crisp, precise separations between bold fields of color.

Printmaking, with its unique balance between spontaneity and structure, has become an extension of Adams's practice. At Tandem Press, Adams has found both a technical and conceptual partner, a space where the collaborative ethos of printmaking aligns seamlessly with our collective commitment to expanding the medium's possibilities. The prints created here are not ancillary to his studio practice; they are integral to it. They echo the collage-based formal language Adams is known for, while pushing the work into new material and expressive territory.

This book is a focused look at Adams's many editions developed at Tandem over a seven-year period. Across these prints, we see Adams's singular celebratory emphasis on pleasure, rest, presentation, and style, filtered through the medium's rich graphic possibilities. Working closely with Tandem's collaborative printers, Adams has taken full advantage of the studio's technical resources and innovative spirit, resulting in prints that pulse with color and rhythm.

What emerges is not only a record of artistic production, but a narrative of creative collaboration, one that underscores the power of printmaking as a democratic and expansive art form. In these prints, Adams continues to construct spaces of affirmation, resistance, and joy that are layered, textured, and vividly expressive.

Eye Candy: Derrick Adams and the Joy of Prints

Judy Hecker

"Sometimes a normal social gathering can represent a radical space."[1]
—Derrick Adams

It was an alluring, unexpected encounter. Up the escalators, into the 2022 International Fine Print Dealers Association Print Fair entrance and, *Bam*. Like everyone around me, I was enveloped by *Eye Candy* (p. 68), a mesmerizing 24-foot long installation of six Pop-inspired prints on psychedelic wallpaper: an explosion of vivid color and serial variation, and a good dose of nostalgic consumerism and sex appeal. Who was this Black man, from decades ago, wearing a form-fitting tank top and underwear, his hands gently resting behind his back? And why was a rainbow swirl lollipop affixed to his eye?

Derrick Adams began his foray into professional printmaking in 2012. He had taken printmaking as an undergraduate studying art education[2] at Pratt Institute in Brooklyn in the 1990s, but it wasn't until he was a visiting artist at Middlebury College in 2012 that he experienced the rush and the possibilities of the collaborative print workshop environment. That experience, plus a commission to create a benefit print for the New York–based nonprofit the Laundromat Project, led Adams to team up with collaborative printer Erik Hougan at the Lower East Side Printshop (LESP) in 2014.

Adams's work with LESP began a deep engagement with the medium. He subsequently published several editions, both individual prints and series, with them. Adams also made prints, based on collage work, beginning in 2015 with Andre Ribouli and Jennifer Mahlman-Ribouli at the state-of-the-art Ribouli Digital in New York, published by Michael Steinberg's Eminence Grise Editions. Adams's engagement with the medium leapt forward in 2019 through an introduction by his close friend, the artist Mickalene Thomas. That was when Adams began what would become his longest sustained printmaking collaboration to date, with Tandem Press, at the University of Wisconsin-Madison.

"As an artist, I've been resistant to the idea of making editions without understanding the purpose or need for it to exist. Thinking about printmaking is a conceptual motivation to me: what would I want to see in multiples, over and over again, that would represent a genuine idea without flattening it out?"[3]

1 Hudson River Museum, *Derrick Adams: Buoyant*, March 7, 2020. https://www.hrm.org/exhibitions/derrick-adams.

2 Adams's degree in art education and his understanding of how children learn by using colors, textures, patterns, and interactive engagement inform the choices he makes in his own artistic practice.

3 Unless otherwise indicated, all quotes by the artist are Derrick Adams, interview by Judy Hecker, in person, Adams's studio, Brooklyn, New York, August 8, 2025.

Prints are part of Adams's broader philosophy about enjoyment, community, access, and democratic collecting. Many collectors of Adams's prints are in their late-20s to mid-30s. They've created a club where anyone can be a member; the prints are almost owned collectively. Adams's print collectors stand in contrast to the more investment-driven audience for his paintings. "Prints are more like, 'Let me see if I can come up with the money for this and own one too,'" he said. Adams commented on how he once loved seeing a collector display a framed print of his next to a rare, collectible sneaker in the home: "I like the idea of people putting different things they appreciate on the same level and displaying them together."

Adams's interest in putting different objects on equal footing, and in the democratic, communal nature of editions, propels his creations. The populist appeal of today's consumer-driven world speaks to Adams, similar to Pop artists who had a pervasive interest in the culture, lifestyle, and consumerism of the 1960s. Pop Art blurred the hierarchy between elite high art, like painting and sculpture, and the immediacy of low art, like comic books, advertising, window displays, and everyday commodities. Printmaking created a bridge between the high and the low, and Adams's work continues to embrace this. The democratic nature of prints and multiples deeply influences Adams, who sees editions as a way of, according to him, "putting images into the world" and "putting art into the hands of people" who may or may not be conventional collectors. His approach is similar to how Andy Warhol and Roy Lichtenstein buttressed their painting practice with prints, wallpaper, placemats, paper plates, and merch. Adams's openness is a forward-thinking and enterprising vision: "I would like to be a part of the future of what art can be," he said.

Adams's creative freedom is captured in a variety of recent, playful projects that fall outside the traditional channels for art. They are collaborative, interactive, and communal by design. In 2025 he created limited-edition printed T-shirts, canvas bags, and posters that channelled New York City summer vibes in a packed pop-up takeover of the cannabis dispensary Gotham Chelsea.[4] On a mass-produced scale, he launched an extensive new JOY collaboration with mega-designer Marc Jacobs, including tote bags, shirts, charm accessories, and a hoodie, which reinterpret Adams's fragmented abstraction-and-dice motif.

Adams also prizes creating multiples in more intimate social spaces, in, for example, spaces where people share meals. His placemat edition, which harks to the artist's early TV-screen works, was a summer 2025 collaboration with Chef Mawa McQueen for their Artist's Table dinner in Aspen; the event reinterpreted the TV dinner concept for invited guests. He does the same

4 The proceeds from sales support the non-profit organization Charm City Cultural Cultivation founded by Adams in Baltimore in 2022 to support and encourage underserved communities in the city through arts, education, and cultural enrichment.

in fine-dining restaurants, too, with a colorful, printed wallpaper mural in celebrity Chef Marcus Samuelsson's newest restaurant in Washington, DC. Adams's numerous benefit prints are tied to special events and dinners that raise funds for and promote the missions of non-profit organizations. They tap into a social context, into human interaction, and into his own direct work with non-profits.[5] At the heart of all these projects is creative expression centered on participation, community, memory, and impact. Prints and multiples are, at their essence, performative for Adams. They connect on a deeper level to his early practice in performance art, where audience and place generated meaning.[6]

Adams collected prints before he committed to making them. He owns prints by Emma Amos, Robert Colescott, Lois Mailou Jones, Jacob Lawrence, Kerry James Marshall, and Nari Ward, some of the greatest artists from the Harlem Renaissance to today. Adams found that his own generation of artists was especially committed to collecting prints. That commitment arose in part due to the medium's affordability, in part because artists see the potential of prints to circulate and market their work more broadly, and in part due to artists' hands-on understanding and appreciation of the complexity of print production. "The print world is more like a gift in some ways, a place where people are able to attain work; it's both another level of visibility for artists and accessibility for the collector." He continued, "Printmaking is not just hitting a button and something comes out of a machine. It's such a unique process and it's really complicated to reproduce a work over and over again."

Once he began making prints in professional workshops, Adams's entire artistic practice evolved. Not coincidentally, after his early printmaking experience at Middlebury College, Adams hired one of the more helpful students as his first studio assistant. This encouraged Adams to communicate and delegate. "You need to be a good communicator to work with printers," he said. Adams came to understand that the physical space of the print workshop, the experience of making art with a collaborative printer, and the experimentation with new creative and material possibilities could inform his artistic development. "Erik [Hougan] was always coming up with the best ways of communicating my ideas into prints. He listened, he gave me challenging feedback, and I found we could be more ambitious together, and push the boundaries, even in that small space of the Lower East Side Printshop. I learned a great deal there," Adams said.

5 Adams was gallery manager and later curatorial director of Rush Arts Gallery, in Chelsea, New York, from 2001 to 2009, before his own career as an artist took off. There, he fostered a platform for early career artists of color in New York and gave early visibility to many artists who would go on to become major figures.

6 For more on Adams' performance art, see Dexter Wimberly, "Black Life, As Lived, Not Constructed," *Derrick Adams* (The Monacelli Press and Gagosian, New York, 2025), 218–237. See also "Derrick Adams | Performance," http://www.derrickadams.com/performance.

Adams brought this formative experience to the spacious and ambitious Tandem Press, where the possibilities seem endless. Artists and printers working "in tandem" is the cornerstone of the workshop's collaborative philosophy. Founded in 1986 by Art Department Faculty, William Weege, on the campus of the University of Wisconsin-Madison, the renowned academic workshop is at the forefront of research and experimentation, and a collaborator with some of the preeminent artists of our time. The press emphasizes education through its affiliation with the Art Department within the School of Education, the hands-on experience it provides students, and its close proximity to the campus's Chazen Museum of Art, which houses the Tandem Press archive.[7] Tandem Press employs three collaborative printmakers—Joe Freye, Jason Ruhl, and Patrick Smyczek—who bring a combined 60 years of experience, each with a particular expertise: etching, relief, screenprint, lithography, photo-intaglio, and digital-hybrid techniques. An experienced group of curators, backed by an enterprising director and dedicated support staff, drive the workshop's relationships with artists and its educational programming. "The combination of Derrick's outgoing nature, level of artistry, and sophisticated intellect is remarkable. As soon as he set foot inside Tandem Press, the chemistry was immediate. Everyone just fell in love with him. And what I admired most was the way he always spoke with the students," said Paula Panczenko, Tandem Press director from 1989 to 2024.[8]

Adams remarked that working at Tandem Press and being outside of New York has taught him to slow down: timing is not as condensed, space is abundant, and there are many specialists to work with. It's a bit "like taking a vacation and making art," he said. Rather unexpectedly, Adams's first project at Tandem Press remains, to this day, his most complex print. "Really good printmakers always want to challenge themselves," he said. These challenges keep Adams on his toes. "The printers will say: 'What do you want to do? Something you haven't done before? We'll figure it out!'"

As it turns out, Freye and Ruhl wanted to put a newly acquired laser engraver to the test. Their first project with Adams, *Self Portrait on Float* (2019) (p. 21), became a puzzle block print composed of 94 individual pieces. The first and largest block printed the blue water; then five more blocks, each containing myriad elements, printed the float and the figure. "It was like a puzzle box with five individual puzzles; each puzzle block contained a bunch of shapes that could be inked and printed up with just one run. Freye explained. "At the time, I would say by far it was the most adventurous thing that we had done," continued Ruhl, "...and we didn't know if it was going to work or not when we started it. It's *a lot* of parts."[9]

7 The Chazen Museum of Art's permanent collection receives one print from every edition that is published by Tandem Press.
8 Paula Panczenko, interview by Judy Hecker, via telephone, Madison, Wisconsin, December 3, 2025.

While at first Adams thought he would make a screenprint, a process more familiar to him, he quickly realized he was "out of [his] league" using the laser engraver to cut woodblocks. And that was okay. Freye and Ruhl broke down Adams's vision into literal pieces while Adams focused on color mixing, compositional devices, and the gold leaf. The artist also added twelve collage elements to create the chain necklace, unicorn horn, teeth, and fingernails. "It was a little panicky in the beginning," Adams recalled. "Every print we do with Derrick pushes us another step or two forward," said Freye.

Adams was hooked: *Boy on Swan Float* (2020) (p. 23), another woodblock with collage, quickly followed. "If I knew that I could do collage on prints, I would probably have done this kind of printmaking from the beginning, from college."[10]

The following two prints, *Party Guest 1* and *2 (We Came to Party and Plan* series*)* (2020–21) (pp. 25, 27), emerged after Adams's summer 2019 residency at the Rauschenberg Foundation. During the residency, he developed a new body of work for a 2020 exhibition at the Hudson River Museum in Yonkers, New York, overlooking the river.[11] Adams noted that Black people couldn't always assemble freely: "We gathered in barber shops, in church, at weddings, and for holidays. These social spaces became political spaces where we could talk freely about everything." At the time of the exhibition, he remarked, "When we get together, it isn't just to have a party. We might be planning a revolution at the same time."[12]

At the Hudson River Museum, Adams created a gallery-sized installation of framed, bust-length and full-length figures—partygoers with hats and blowers—made with fabric and paper collage. These were installed above wall collages of patterned tablecloths and benches inspired by West African fabric, polka dots, and stripes. Both representational and actual party pennants and balloons surrounded white picnic tables. Simulated cinderblock walls, windows, and DJ equipment completed the *mise-en-scène*. Adams added four wall sculptures, *Tables Turned* (2016), created to the actual scale of a party table and collaged with utensils, paper plates, cups, and placemats.[13] During the opening celebration, attendees wore actual party hats and danced, filling the room with joy and mimicking their artistic counterparts on the walls.

9 Unless otherwise indicated, all quotes by the printers are Joe Freye, Jason Ruhl, and Patrick Smyczek, interview by Judy Hecker, via Zoom, Tandem Press, Madison, Wisconsin, July 31, 2025.

10 IFPDA Print Fair, "Eye Candy: Derrick Adams in Conversation with Jennifer Farrell," October 30, 2022. https://www.youtube.com/watch?v=MWjAlikwBqU&t=3s.

11 The exhibition *Derrick Adams: We Came to Party and Plan* was on view at the Hudson River Museum, Yonkers, New York, March 7–October 18, 2020, and overlapped with Adams's Hudson River Museum exhibition *Derrick Adams: Buoyant*, March 7–August 23, 2020.

12 Hudson River Museum, *Derrick Adams: We Came to Party and Plan*, March 7, 2020. https://www.hrm.org/exhibitions/we-came-to-party-and-plan/.

Two of the unique bust-length figures Adams made during his Rauschenberg residency and incorporated into the Hudson River Museum exhibition inspired the two prints *Party Guest 1* and *2* that followed. When beginning a print project, Adams and the printers looked for fresh approaches to moving from one medium to another. Adams also decided to take the unique works out of circulation and keep them for himself, an act he often does to prioritize the prints.

For *Party Guest 1* and *2*, Adams manipulated the original compositions and created new colors, skin tones, and patterns. He also flipped the orientation so that the male and female figures would face each other, as if engaging in conversation or revelry. He sourced new materials: the readymade clothing fabric used in the unique collages was reinterpreted using bookcloth sourced in Italy for the prints. Bookcloth is typically used for book covers and spines and "it's already archival, paper-backed, and not so textured that you can't print well on it," explained Smyczek, who had used bookcloth in his own work as an artist. "We had never done it before at Tandem but it was the right thing for the project." The background shapes and figures in the prints are rendered using screenprint, a technique that favors areas of flat color, while the party hats were relief printed with a vintage Vandercook press using relief plates. The prints can be displayed either as a pair or individually. Appearing frozen in motion—a mouth agape, a wide smile—these block-like figures are joyful symbols of everyday Black life, and stand as monuments to powerful gatherings, past and present.

The print series *Style Variations* (pp. 51–67) followed in two parts in 2020 and 2023, based on photographs of female mannequin heads Adams had been casually shooting for years in storefront beauty and wig shops around his Brooklyn neighborhood. This body of work reflects Adams's interest in glamour, portraiture, resourcefulness, and consumerism. "Some look shabby, some look cool. I learned a lot of stuff. The young Black women working at these places cut and style the hair and style the mannequin heads. They create a visual culture that entices other women to come in and buy stuff," Adams said. He would frequent these beauty supply stores to document their changing windows and DIY styles, some of which now have elaborate names and price tags to match. He wanted to elevate this form of cultural production and capture it as art. He did so, at first, by creating large-scale works on paper in 2018 and then monumental eight-foot tall paintings in 2019 and 2020 that combined digital printing and overpainting by hand. These epic figures float on stark white backgrounds; their geometric faces, inspired partly by the designs of West African masks, are topped with brightly colored dip-dyed wigs, some with LGBTQ pride flag colors.

13 *Tables Turned* (2016) were first exhibited in *Derrick Adams: Culture Club* at the Project for Empty Space, Newark, New Jersey, May 18–June 24, 2016, alongside works from his *Floater* series.

When he arrived at Tandem Press in 2019 to transform the empowering work from his *Beauty World* series into prints, Adams expanded the theme by creating a series of four male versions of the mannequins that existed mainly as female versions in his photography and paintings. In 2022 he returned to Tandem Press to create five prints of female mannequins with newly invented hair styles; each title contains a description, such as "Pixie," "Space Buns," and "Side Part." To produce the prints, Adams painted on digital printouts of various mannequin heads with geometric forms that comprise their varied skin tones, makeup, and hairstyles. These provided mock-ups for the printers to reference. In the prints, the bold hair color of the paintings is replaced by black and gray tones that emphasize the creativity of the hair designs, while the skin tones have greater contrast and emphasize their cubist qualities.

Adams's newest print from the *Beauty World* series, *Where My Girls At?* (2024) (p. 19), presents a group of four mannequins on display together in a storefront window. It is a remarkable 62-color screenprint. The viewer's vantage point is from within the store; through the window we see cars on the street in the background. Unlike the steely gazes and overt mannequin heads of the *Style Variation* series, the softer gaze and head tilt of this central figure are more lifelike, as are her interactions with both the viewer and the other mannequins—a human dynamic at the heart of Adams's work. The title of the print *Where My Girls At?* is taken from a 1999 song (and video) by the R&B group 702, which became an international hit, especially among Black female listeners.[14]

While varied gazes define *Style Variations*, no faces are found in Adams's four prints *Parlay 1–4* (pp. 37–43), also created in 2024. "It was a more experimental and different kind of project," Freye said. The compositions shift between abstraction and representation, evoking a truncated figure moving and turning as if walking on a fashion runway. The prints are an outgrowth of Adams's *Mood Board* works, inspired by the famous Black fashion designer Patrick Kelly (1954–1990).[15] Kelly was known for his exuberant and humorous designs embellished with oversized bows, hearts, buttons, and dice.[16] Adams had been researching Kelly for an *inHarlem* project presented by the Studio Museum in Harlem, in partnership with the Schomburg Center for Research in Black Culture, and the New York Public Library's Countee Cullen branch.[17] Kelly's rich fabrics, vivid geometric forms, and form-fitting dresses spoke to Adams, as did the designer's whimsical play, Southern roots, Black memorabilia collection, and nightclub and runway culture. Adams was especially inspired by Kelly's printed dice pattern from the late 1980s.

14 In 2023, 702 performed "Where My Girls At?" in tribute to Missy Elliott (who wrote the song alongside other artists), an honoree at the televised 8th Black Music Honors.

15 Kelly was the first American designer admitted into the Chambre Syndicale du Prêt-à-Porter des Couturiers et des Créateurs de Mode, France's prestigious association of designers, whose members have included Yves Saint Laurent, Sonia Rykiel, and Kelly's sponsor, Christian Lacroix.

For the prints, Adams first experimented with the bold patterns and vivid colors of his *Mood Board* series, as well as with stripes and polka dots. He also took cues from his 2022 print *Silver Lining* (p. 29), created with Tandem Press to support EXPO CHICAGO, which incorporates a vintage clothing pattern and plays with perspective by presenting the lining and structure of a coat from the vantage point beneath the fashion runway.

For *Parlay 1–4*, Adams ultimately chose a palette of browns and grays to articulate skin tones. He also dropped the stripes and dots, and instead leaned into Kelly's dice motif. Having worked with bookcloth on *Party Guest 1* and 2, the printers knew that the dice pattern could be screenprinted on bookcloth to simulate the look and feel of fabric. Adams maintained the sewing-pattern design and the printers determined that the "vanilla-looking paper" of the pattern pieces would be better printed with archival inkjet, having learned from a prior print of Adams's.

The long zippers, which suggest clothing opening and closing around the figure, also went through a process of development. Initially Adams wanted actual zippers, but that was not practical for sheets of paper. Instead, "Ruhl found a way to interpret the zipper," Adams said. Ruhl purchased zippers from a local fabric store and scanned them to create the screenprinted zippers using reflective silver ink that maintained the look of a real zipper. All the elements were then cut out and collaged onto paper that had been screenprinted with the flat shapes of browns and grays. Smyczek recalled: "I had already worked with Derrick on several projects, so his color palette was very familiar to me. I typically save color samples from Derrick's previous prints and use those as a starting point. Some of the brown shades used in *Parlay* were from previous prints, others I newly mixed based on what Derrick described to me. I do a lot of testing so the artist can see what a color looks like in relation to other colors. Mixing color is one of my favorite parts of the job."

The resulting prints have a rich and varied surface quality. "[*Parlay*] mirrors my practice as an artist in the way you experiment with materials through papers, embellishments, texture, and things mixing around," Adams said. The works also show Adams's ongoing interest in manipulating the illusion of space.

The word "parlay" in the work's title is associated with games and gambling, and refers to a bet that links multiple wagers together and offers higher potential winnings. It is a term used in some board games involving dice. In vernacular, "parlay" also means to relax, chill, and have leisurely discussion.

16 Fine Arts Museum of San Francisco, *Patrick Kelly: Runway of Love*, October 23, 2021. https://www.famsf.org/exhibitions/patrick-kelly.

17 Studio Museum in Harlem, *Derrick Adams: Patrick Kelly*, The Journey, May 3, 2017. https://www.studiomuseum.org/exhibitions/derrick-adams-patrick-kelly-the-journey.

Adams's four *Parlay* prints tap into the various meanings of the word, particularly with their dice motif and playful references to Patrick Kelly's own whimsy.

Eye Candy (p. 68) was published by Tandem Press in 2023 but originated with an idea Adams had while working years earlier with Erik Hougan at the Lower East Side Printshop. Hougan even printed proofs, but the ambition Adams had in mind for the project was too great for LESP, so he tabled it.[18] Adams resurrected the concept when he was invited by the International Fine Print Dealers Association to create a large-scale, site-specific project for the entrance to the 2022 print fair at the River Pavilion in New York's Javits Center. He immediately knew Tandem Press would be right for its production.

"*Eye Candy* pushed us, due to how big the final scale was, utilizing a tiny image," Ruhl acknowledged. The work is based on a seemingly banal advertisement from a vintage *Ebony* magazine of the late 1960s or early 1970s for an underwear company; the pixelated figure was no more than two inches in height. The model is shown wearing different muted color underwear "with printed names that were like flavors," Adams described. Although small in scale, this anonymous, muscled figure held a gaze that commanded enormous, provocative presence. Adams envisioned the model larger and in vivid colors that put his quietly radical, confrontational stance at lifescale. "What drew me to the work is the provocative image, and the original flavor labels presented a kind of experience of smell or taste or familiarity. Maybe we can do that with color and achieve the same thing. Take the words away and replace them with bold color and big scale," Adams said.

To start the project, Adams got the original scan of the advertisement from Hougan and began transforming it into a new work at Tandem Press. Adams had Andy Warhol and Sol LeWitt prints at the forefront while he thought about serial repetition and color variation. Smyczek recalled, "The apparel colors for *Eye Candy* were the only variations from print to print. I mixed these colors with very saturated inks and then modified them with a transparent screenprinting base. This resulted in colors with the right amount of 'pop,' but also a vintage sensibility."

Unlike the typically smooth, saturated color of Adams's screenprints, this series exaggerates the dot pattern of the original newspaper clip. Mass media in the 1960s used inexpensive mechanical printing methods: a halftone process to produce a continuous-tone image with a dot pattern,

18 Erik Hougan, interview by Judy Hecker, via telephone, Brooklyn, New York, August 18, 2025.

and the Ben-Day dot process often used in comic books and popularized by Roy Lichtenstein's iconic method. *Eye Candy* harks back to the enlarged, appropriated erotica of the Pop aesthetic, seen in works like Richard Hamilton's muscled male figure in the screenprint *Adonis in Y Fronts* (1963), based on an advertisement in a body-building magazine, or Gerald Laing's series of six screenprints of bikini-clad figures in *Baby, Baby, Wild Things & Brigitte Bardot* (1968), based on mass-media images. Adams's *Eye Candy* blends a powerful critique and celebration of the Pop aesthetic and ideals of beauty, gender, race, sexuality, and desire. Peering around the flavored lollipop, Adams's male figure both invites our gaze and holds his own space and agency.

Eye Candy's placement at the entrance to the print fair put viewers in direct confrontation with the blown-up imagery, further amplifying its impact. LeWitt's immersive, large-scale wall drawings[19] partly informed Adams's decision to set the six life-size prints on wallpaper that referenced the lollipop and the proverbial "eye candy." It was the first time that Tandem integrated wallpaper into a project. The printers contacted Twenty2, a wallpaper and textiles company known for their collaborative, custom work.[20] Adams envisioned the prints set against a magnified detail of the lollipop that looks like a rainbow when installed.[21] Together, the artist, printers, and wallpaper designers made it happen.

"The trust between us and the artist has only gotten stronger. But the magic has not gone away for Derrick. He is still like a kid in a candy store," the Tandem Press printers all agreed. "The relationship was easy from the beginning and it has gotten deeper over time," explained Freye. "There's a very real affection on both sides."

This trust and affection, which often develop between artists and printers in the close-knit environment of the print workshop, connect to the joy that Adams experiences through artmaking and, especially, printmaking. He revels in the joy of inventing, the joy of collaborating, and the joy of knowing that his work is being viewed and collected in a powerfully accessible way. It is a covert political act of spreading images of Black joy and culture far and wide.

19 Adams directly engaged with a Sol LeWitt wall drawing in his September 9, 2016, performance *Derrick Adams: Finding Derrick 6 to 8* at the Metropolitan Museum of Art, New York. He performed for two hours in front of the wall drawing while wearing a custom-designed suit based on Sol LeWitt's 1982 *Wall Drawing #370: Ten Geometric Figures (including right triangle, cross, X, diamond) with three-inch parallel bands of lines in two directions)*.

20 Adams's first collaboration with Twenty2, located in Naugatuck, Connecticut, was on a custom wallpaper project for the exhibition *Derrick Adams: Interior Life* at Luxembourg + Co., New York, February 26–April 20, 2019.

21 When *Eye Candy* is purchased, the prints come with the licensing rights to print the custom wallpaper as needed in perpetuity.

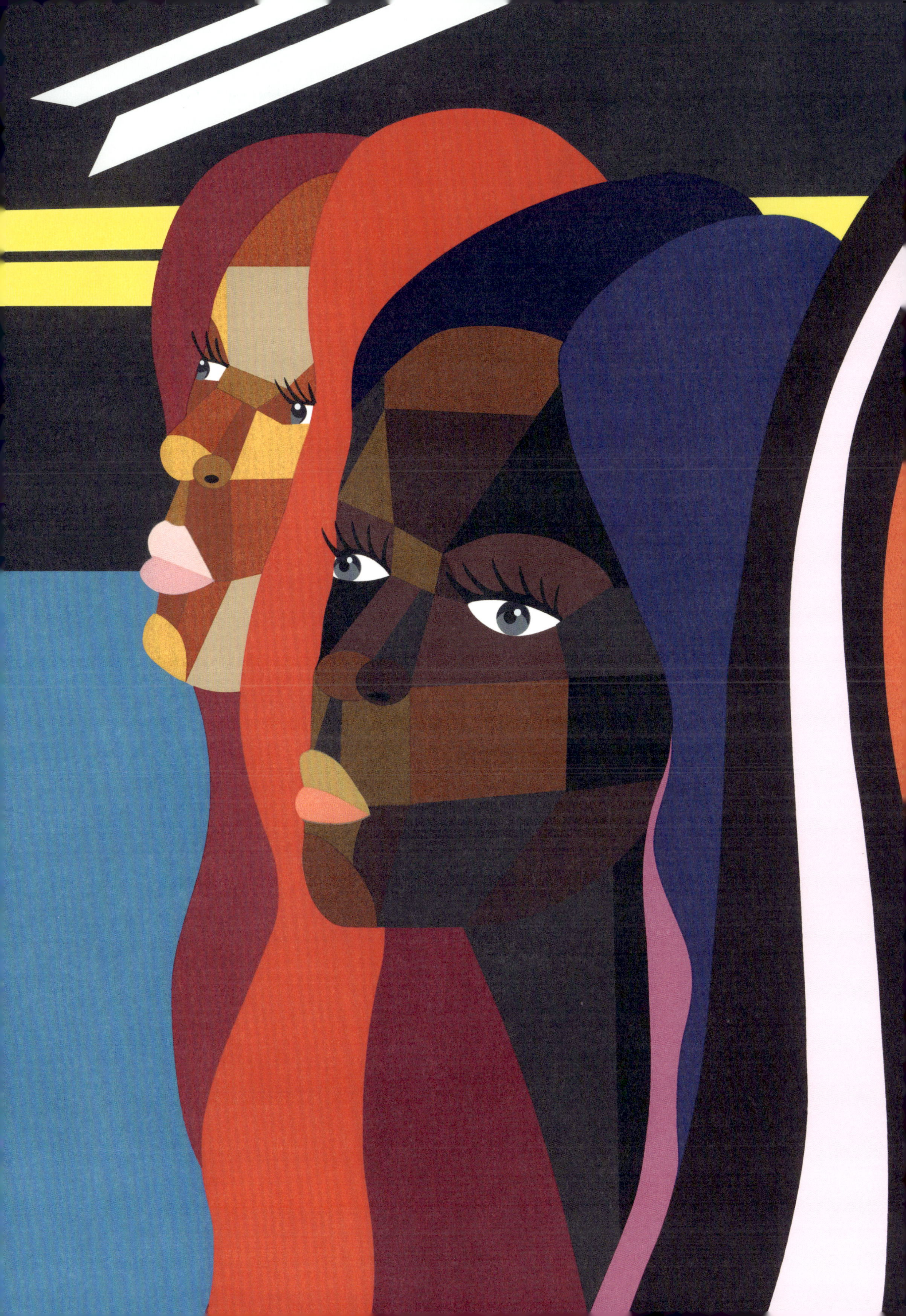

Where My Girls At?, 2024
Screenprint on Lanaquarelle. Edition of 40. 36 × 36 inches.

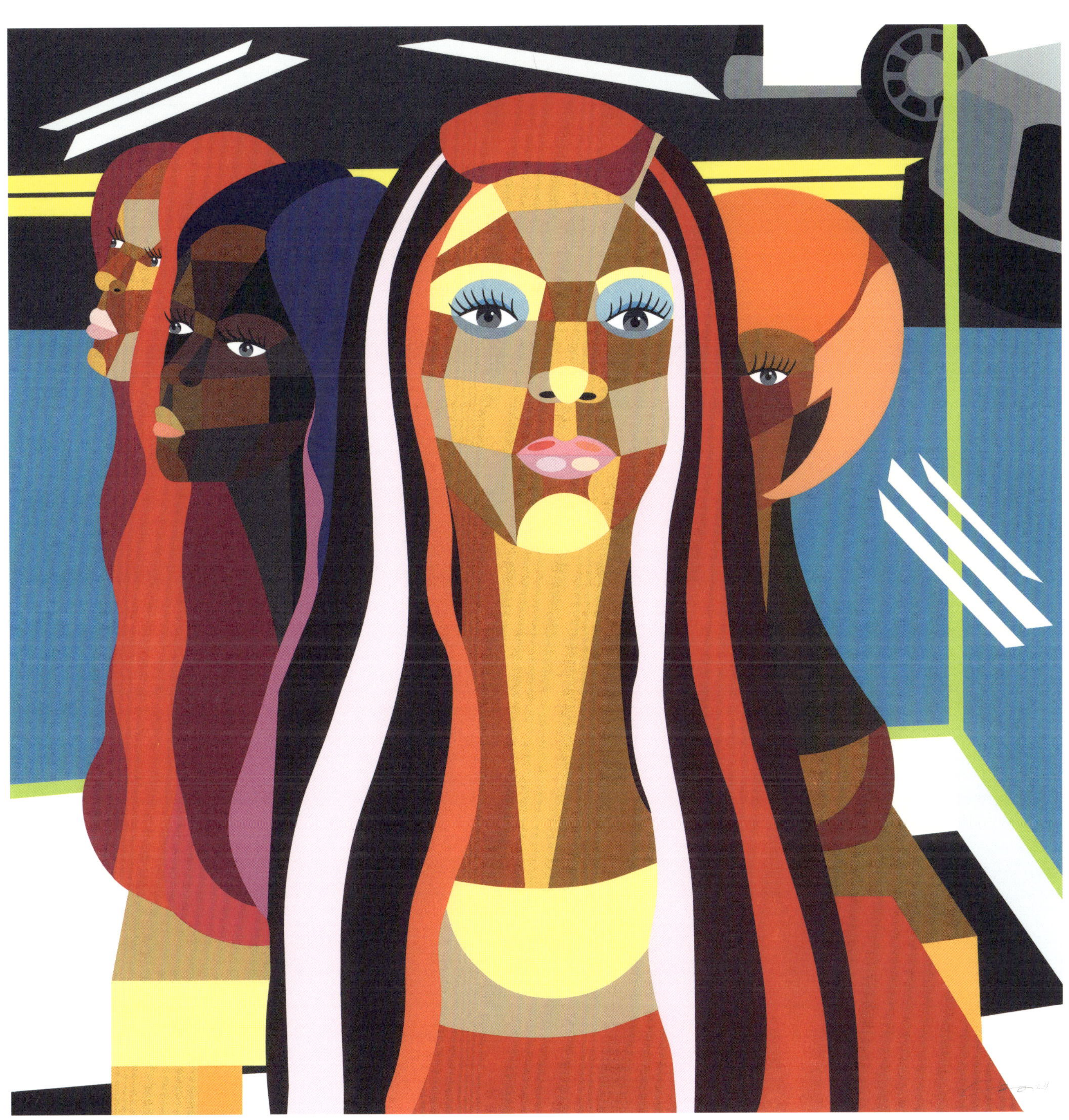

Self Portrait on Float, 2019
Woodblock, gold leaf, and collage on Rives BFK with Kitakata Natural and Canson Ti-Meintes. Edition of 50. 40 × 40 inches.

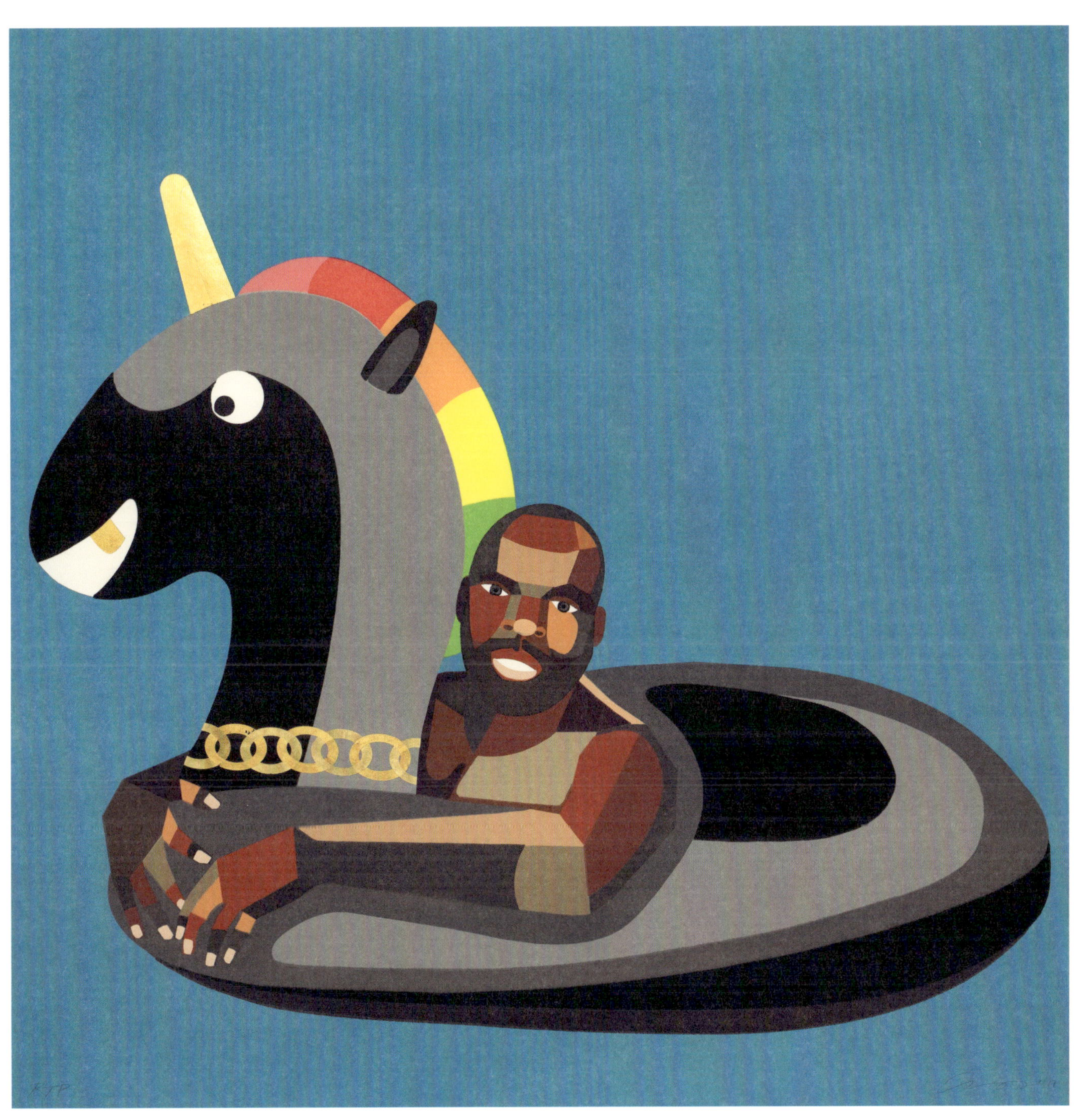

Boy on Swan Float, 2020
Woodblock, screenprint, and collage on Iris Bookcloth
and Rives BFK. Edition of 30. 31 × 45 inches.

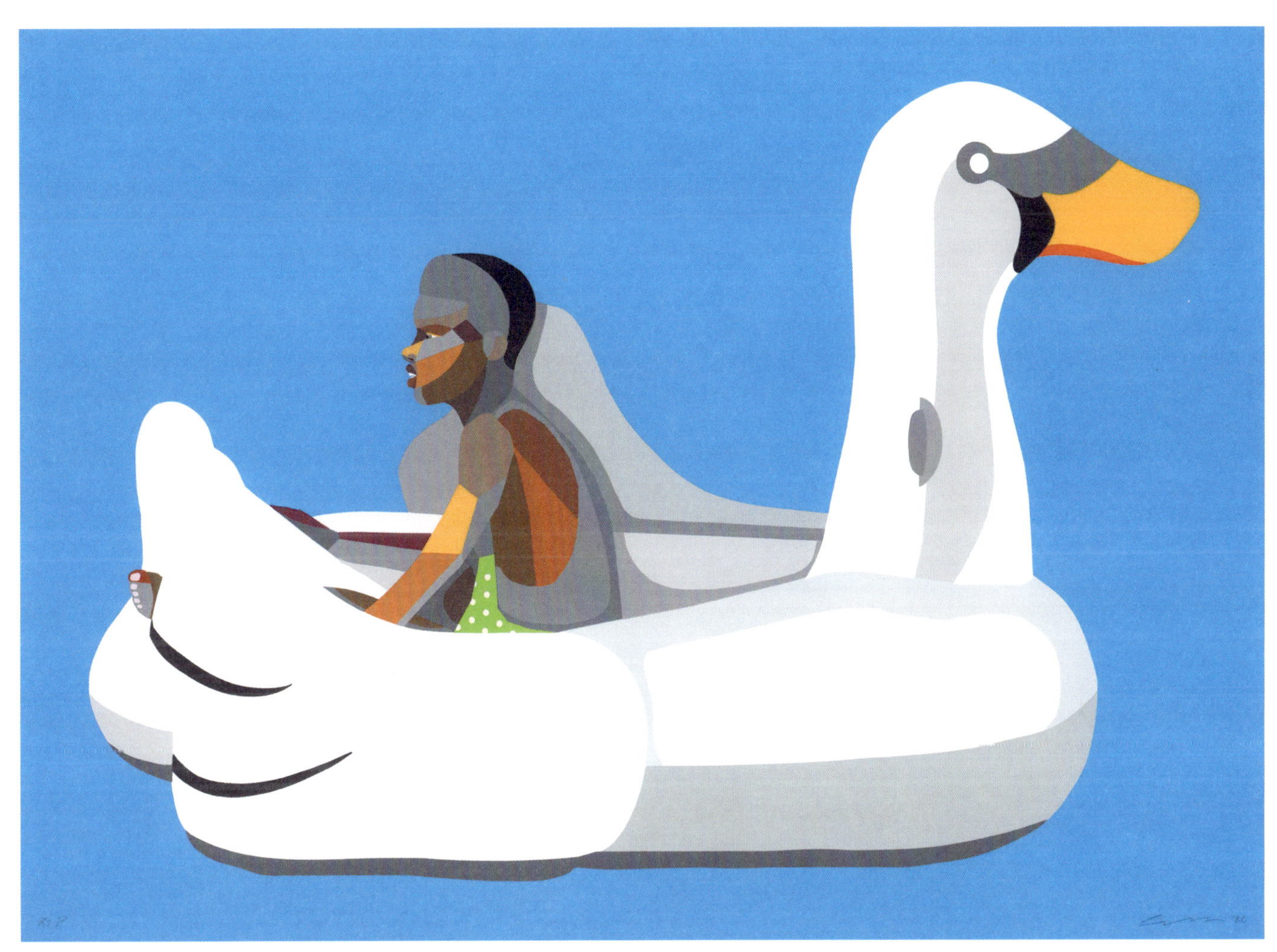

Party Guest 1 (We Came to Party and Plan Series), 2020
Screenprint, relief, and collage on Iris Bookcloth,
Arches 88, and Rives BFK. Edition of 50. 24 × 18 inches.

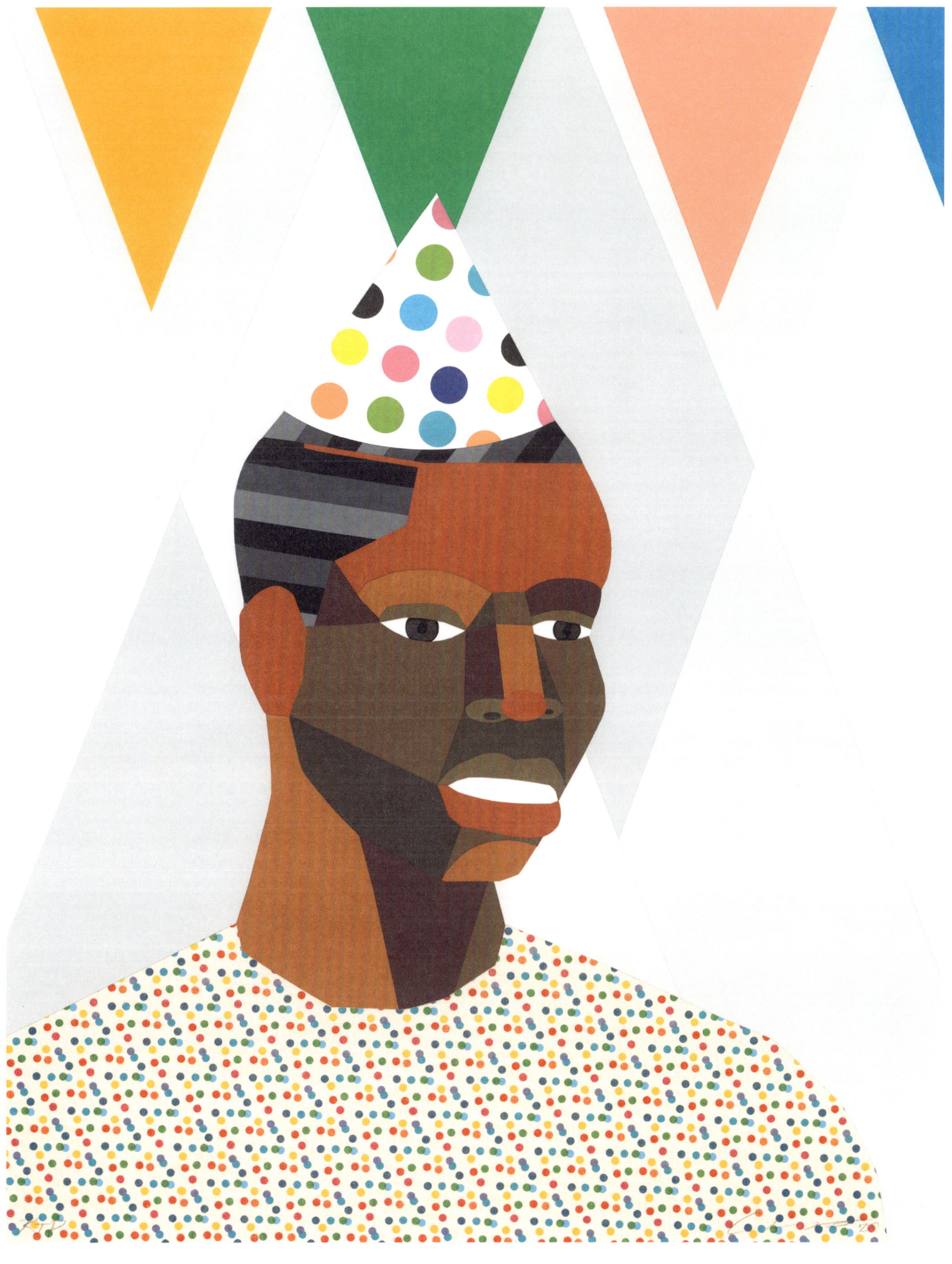

Party Guest 2 (We Came to Party and Plan Series), 2021
Screenprint, relief, and collage on Iris Bookcloth, Arches 88, and Rives BFK. Edition of 50. 24 × 18 inches.

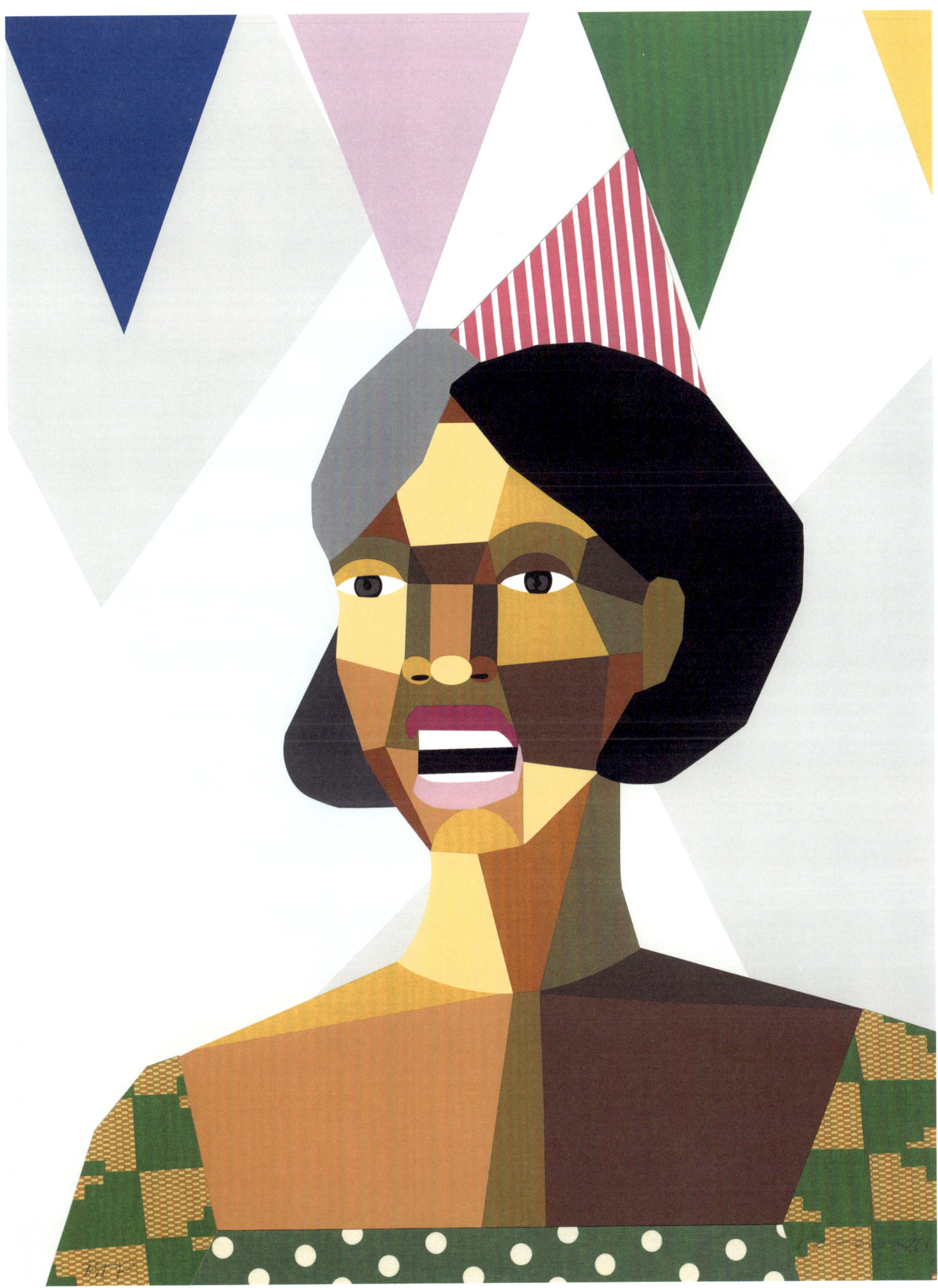

Silver Lining, 2024
Screenprint, relief, and collage on Arches 88 and
Somerset Book White. Edition of 100. 27 ½ × 20 inches.

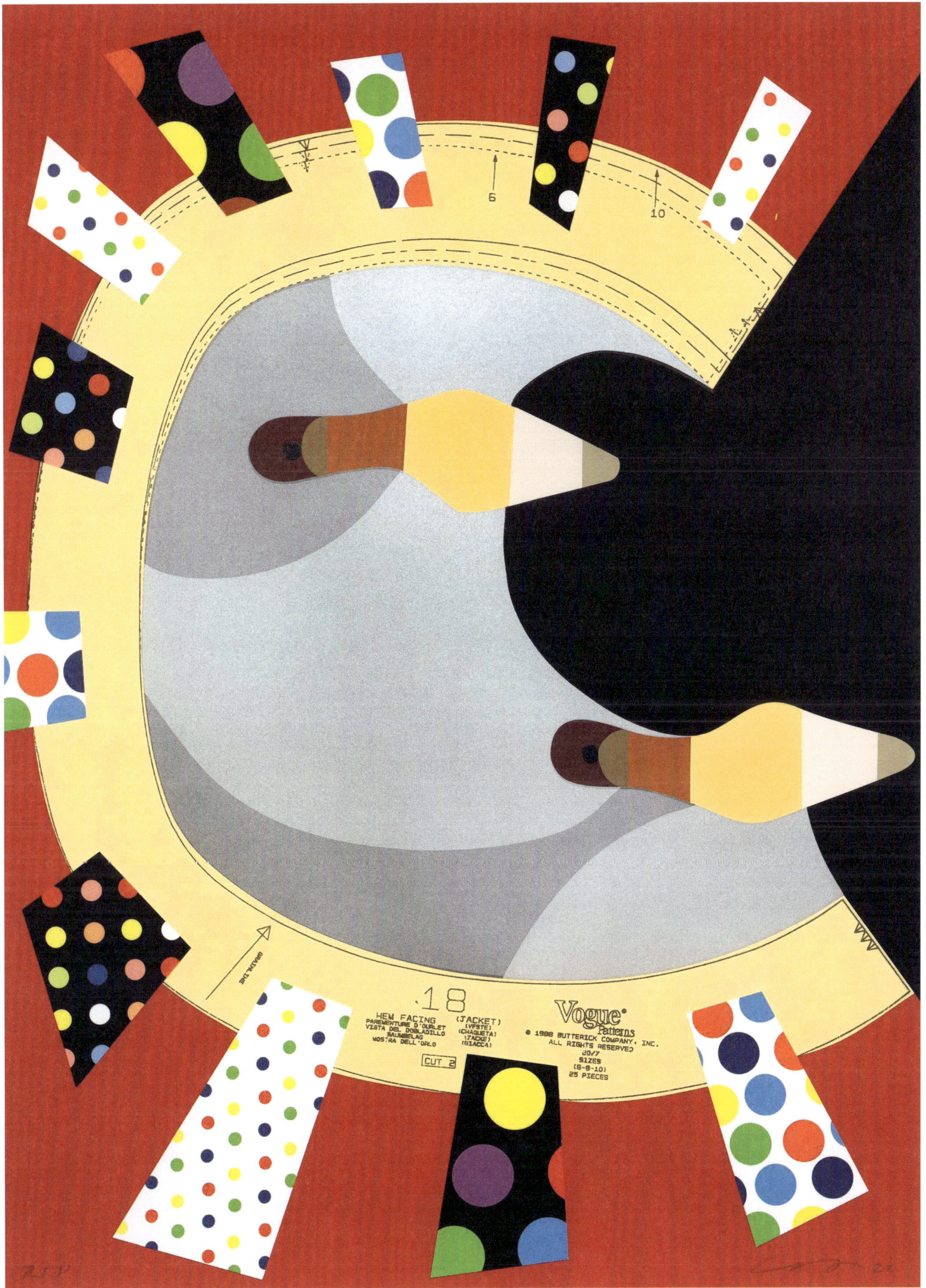
6
10
GRAINLINE
18
HEM FACING
PAREMENTURE D'OURLET
VISTA DEL DOBLADILLO
SAUMBELAG
MOSTRA DELL'ORLO
(JACKET)
(VESTE)
(CHAQUETA)
(JACKE)
(GIACCA)
CUT 2
Vogue® Patterns
© 1988 BUTTERICK COMPANY, INC.
ALL RIGHTS RESERVED
20/7
SIZES
(6-8-10)
25 PIECES

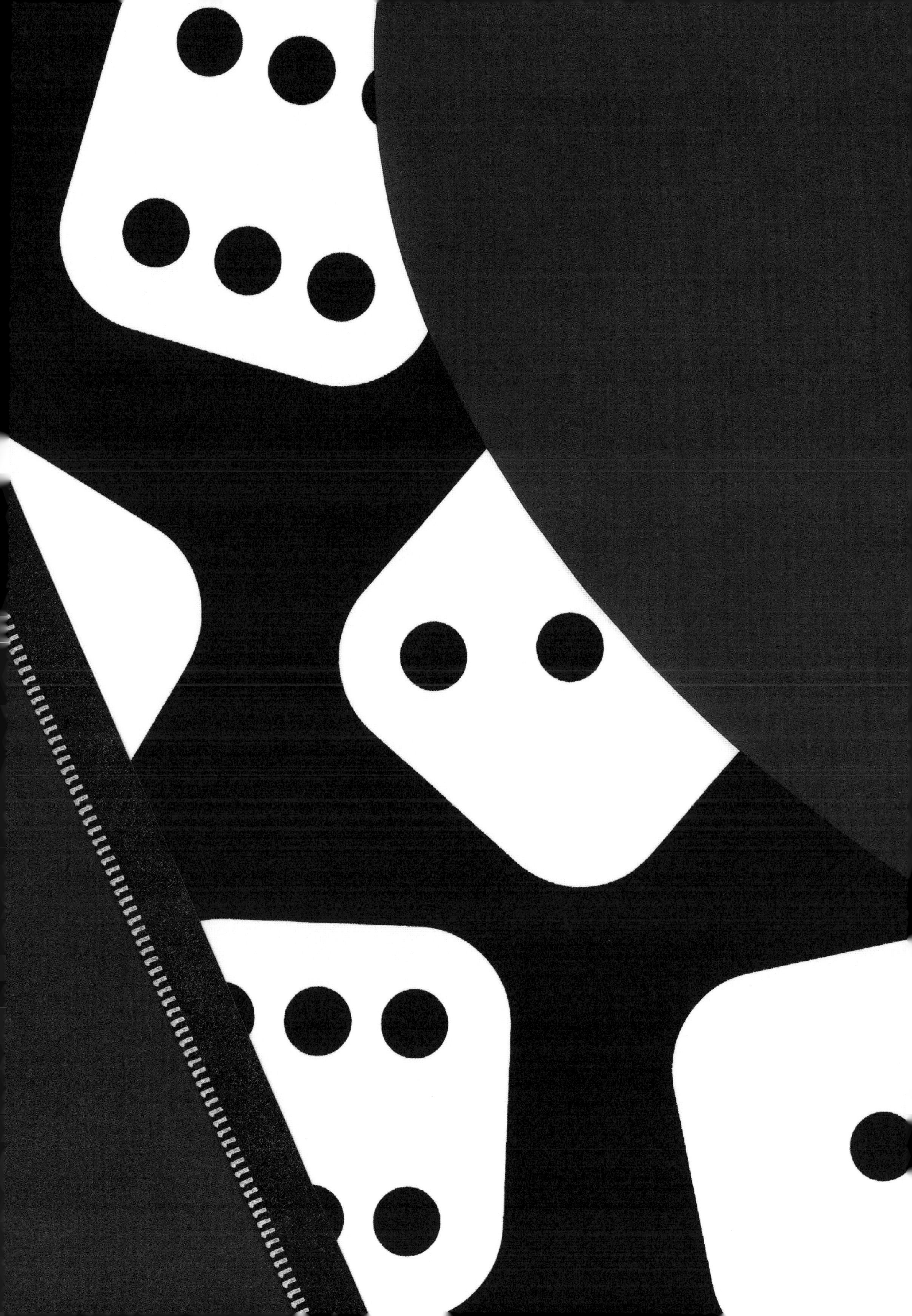

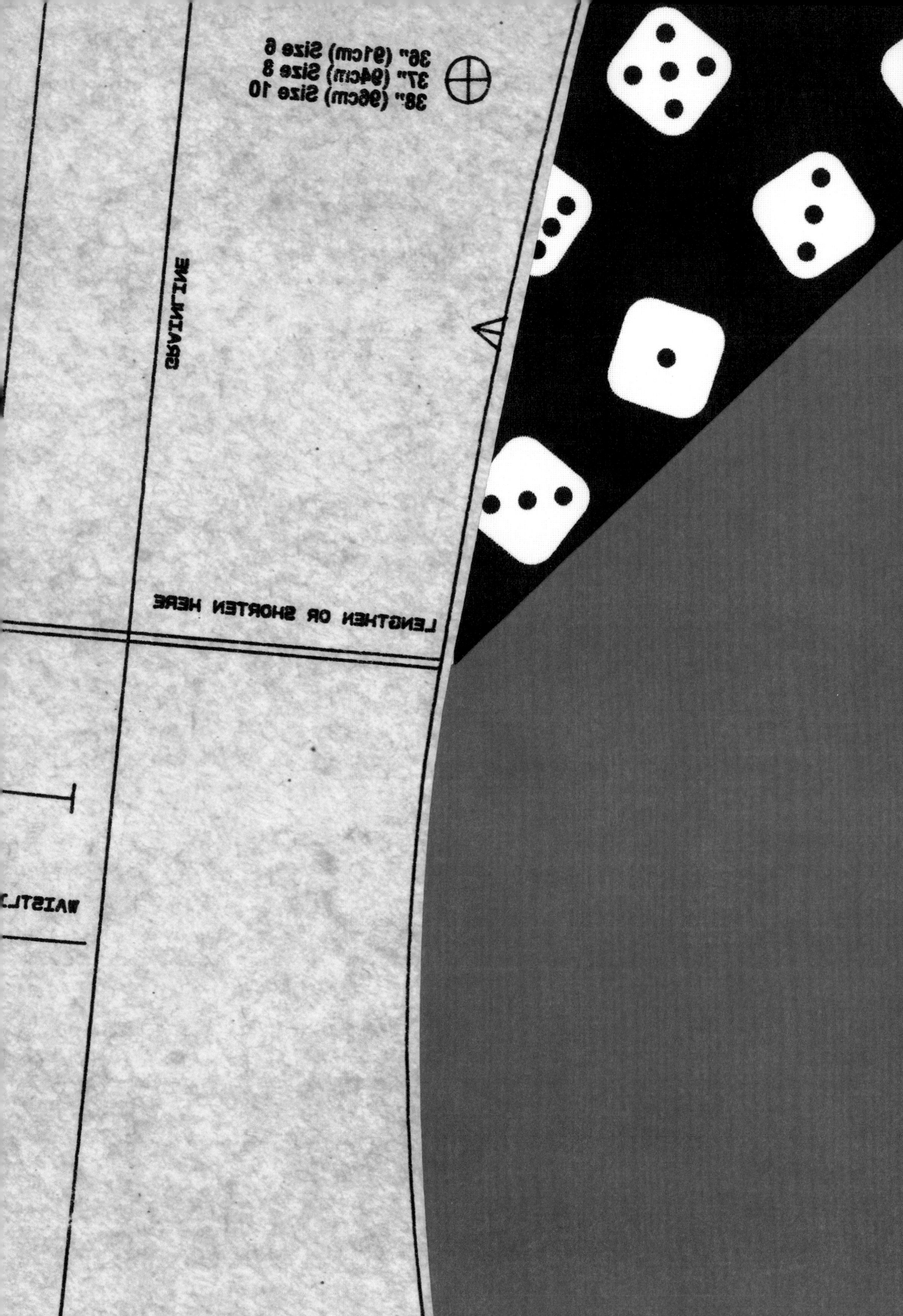
36" (91cm) Size 6
37" (94cm) Size 8
38" (96cm) Size 10
GRAINLINE
LENGTHEN OR SHORTEN HERE

Parlay 1-4
After Derrick Adams & Patrick Kelly

by Krista Franklin

1.

The city streets are a runway
of form, arrows of arms
pointing in every direction.

2.

Mississippi genius stitches
from south to Saint Laurent.
A tissue thin pattern to Paris.

3.

In the tucks of the boulevard
brown free forms gather and change
alleys into catwalks of currency.

4.

Dice scatter across the curve
of ready-to-wear print, a gamble
of couture, unzipped, elegant.

p. 30: *Parlay 4*, 2024 (detail)
Opposite and previous page: *Parlay 1*, 2024 (detail)

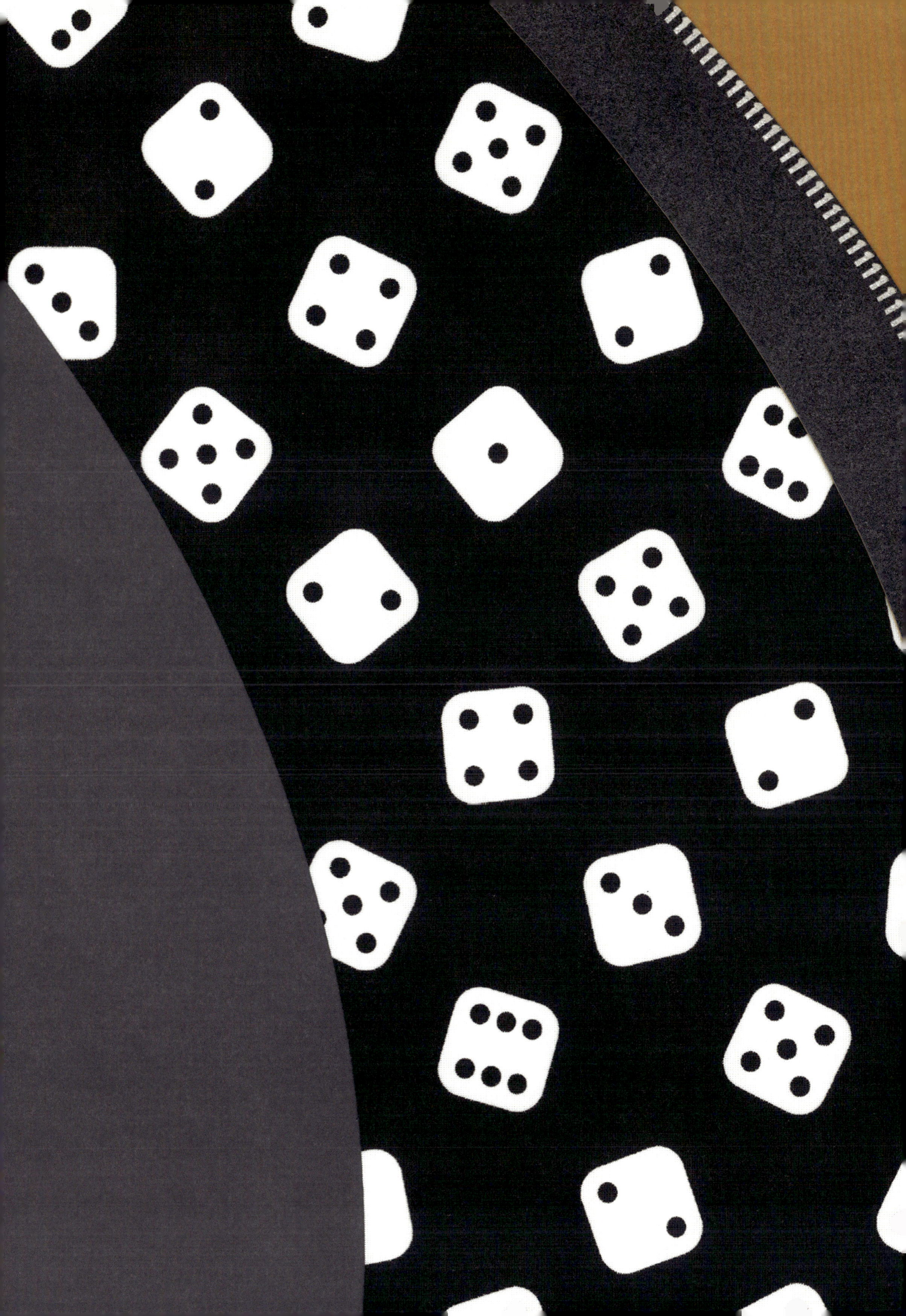

Parlay 1, 2024
Screenprint, archival inkjet, and collage on Lanaquarelle with
Iris Bookcloth, Kozo, and Arches 88. Edition of 30. 36 × 24 inches.

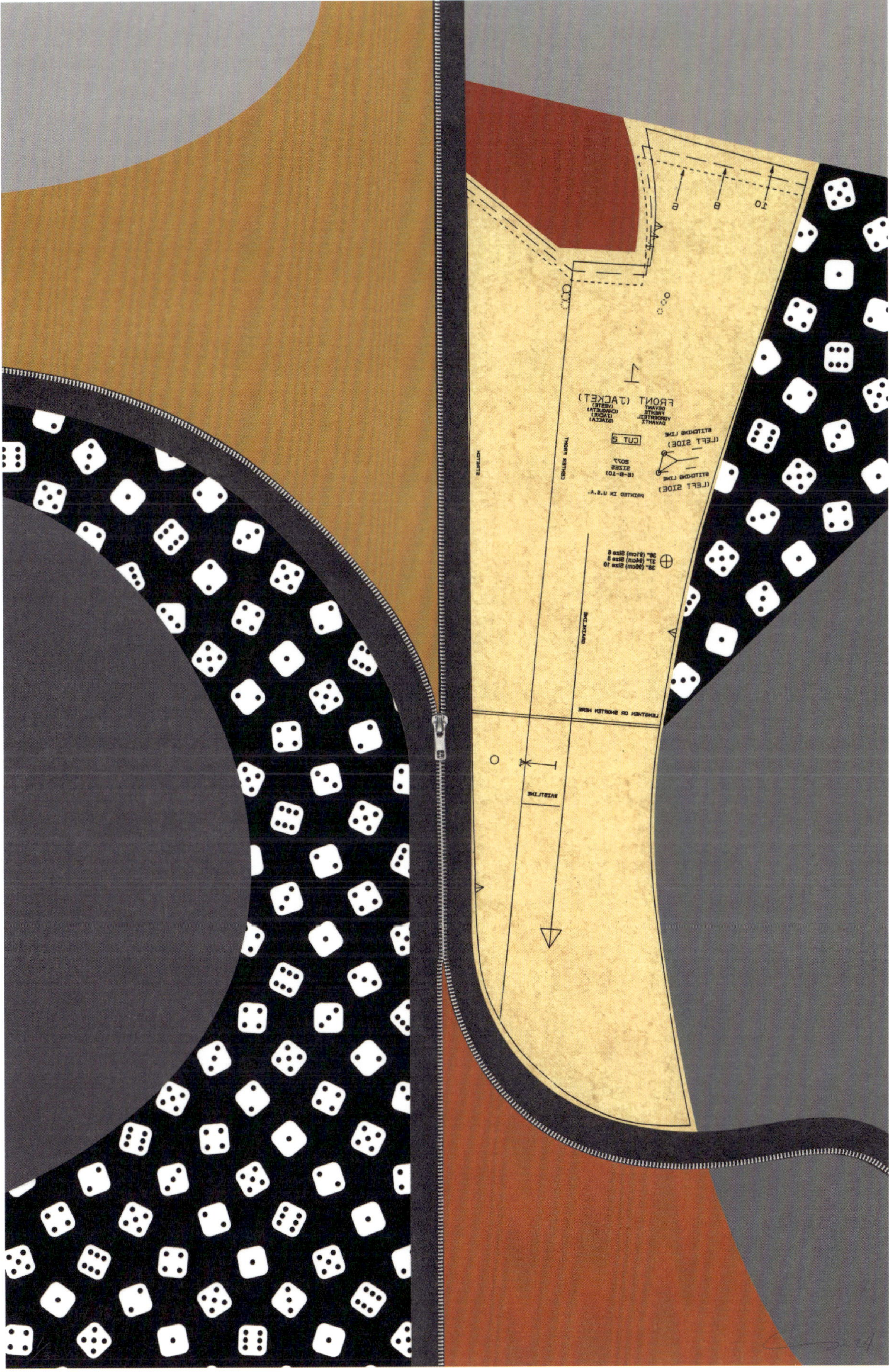

Parlay 2, 2024
Screenprint, archival inkjet, and collage on Lanaquarelle with
Iris Bookcloth, Kozo, and Arches 88. Edition of 30. 36 × 24 inches.

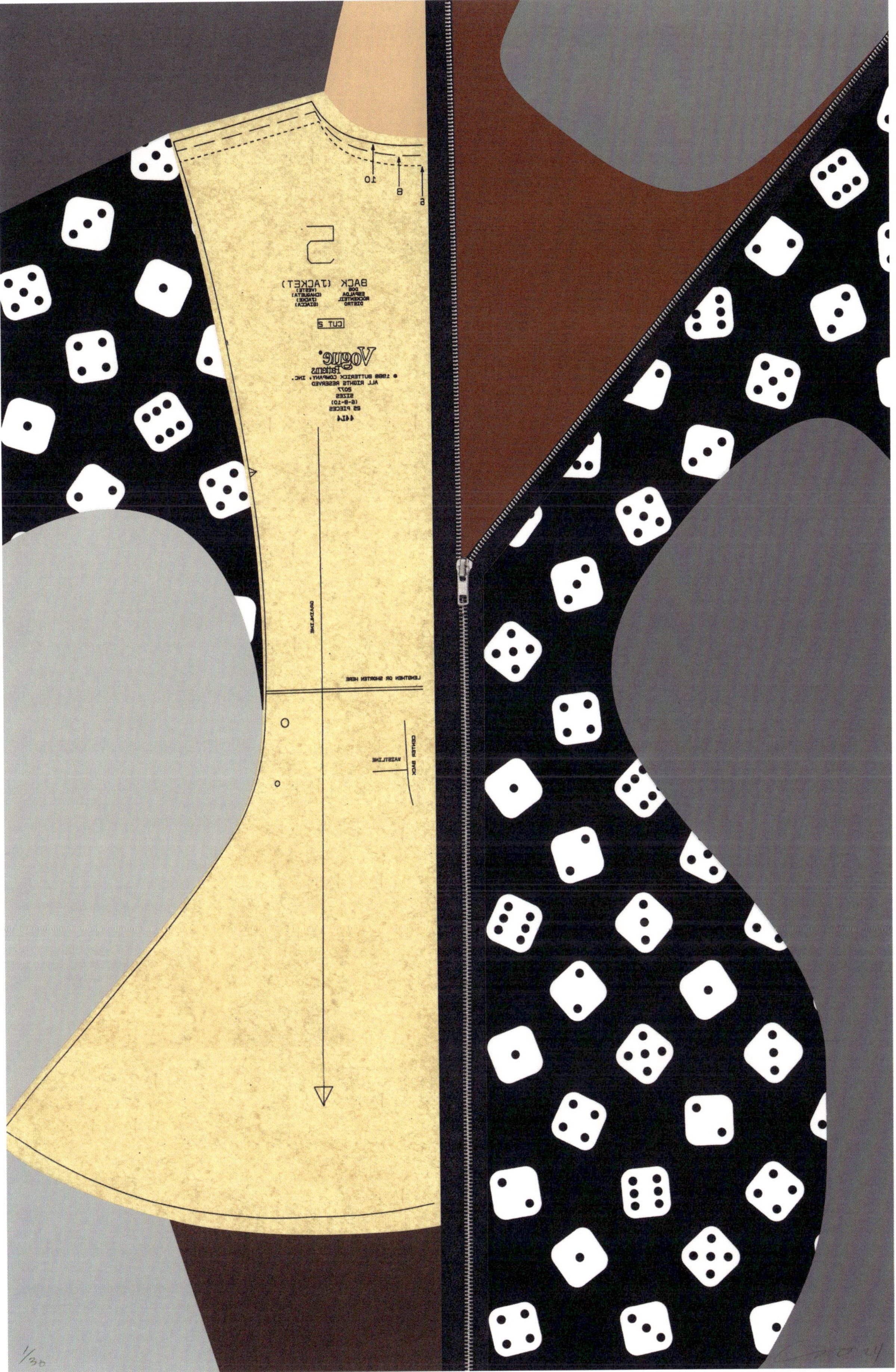
1/30

Parlay 3, 2024
Screenprint, archival inkjet, and collage on Lanaquarelle with
Iris Bookcloth, Kozo, and Arches 88. Edition of 30. 36 × 24 inches.

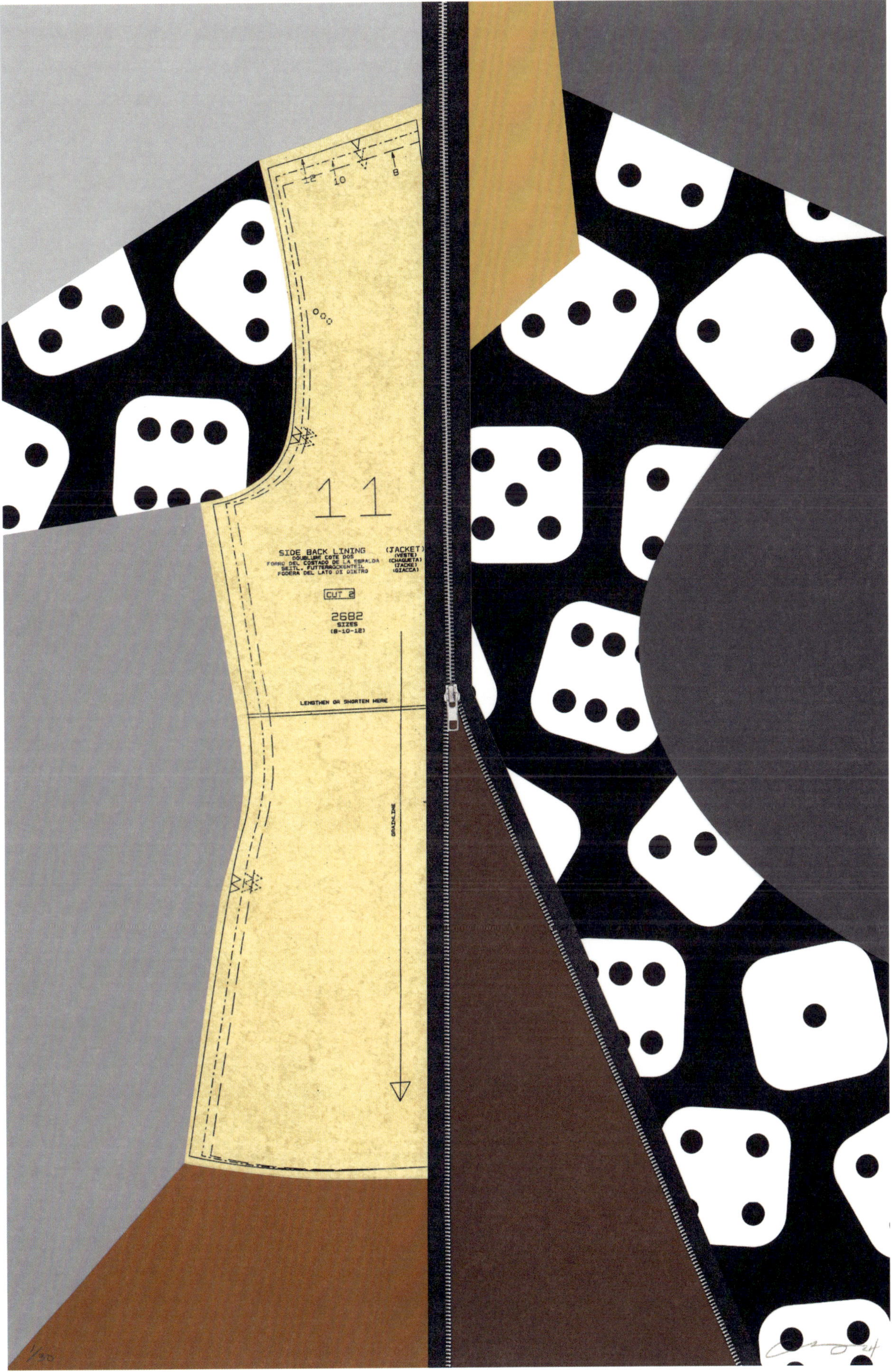
12
10
8
11
SIDE BACK LINING (JACKET)
DOUBLURE COTE DOS (VESTE)
FORRO DEL COSTADO DE LA ESPALDA (CHAQUETA)
SEITL. FUTTERRÜCKENTEIL (JACKE)
FODERA DEL LATO DI DIETRO (GIACCA)
CUT 2
2682
SIZES
(8-10-12)
LENGTHEN OR SHORTEN HERE
GRAINLINE
1/30

Parlay 4, 2024
Screenprint, archival inkjet, and collage on Lanaquarelle with
Iris Bookcloth, Kozo, and Arches 88. Edition of 30. 36 × 24 inches.

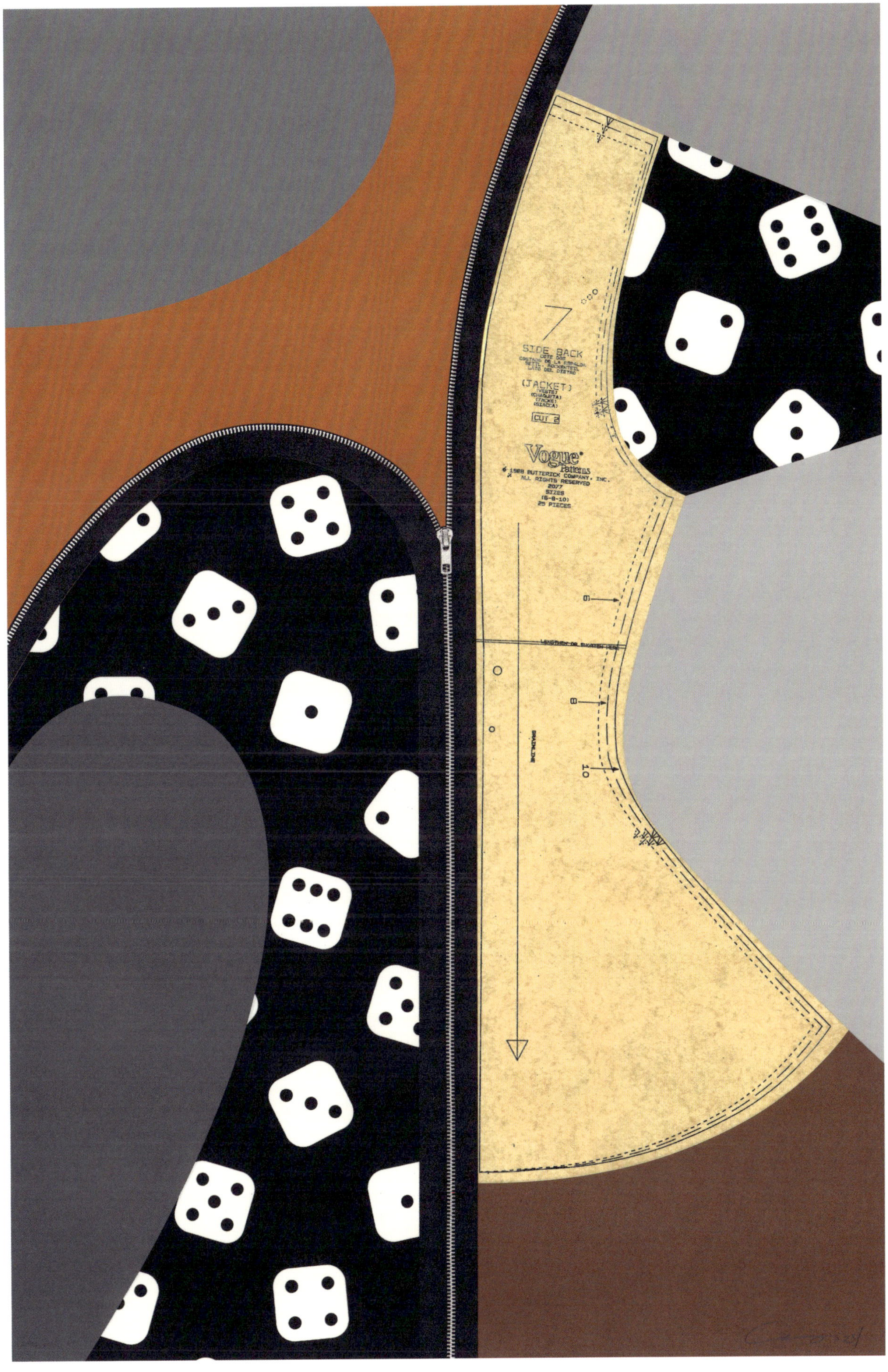

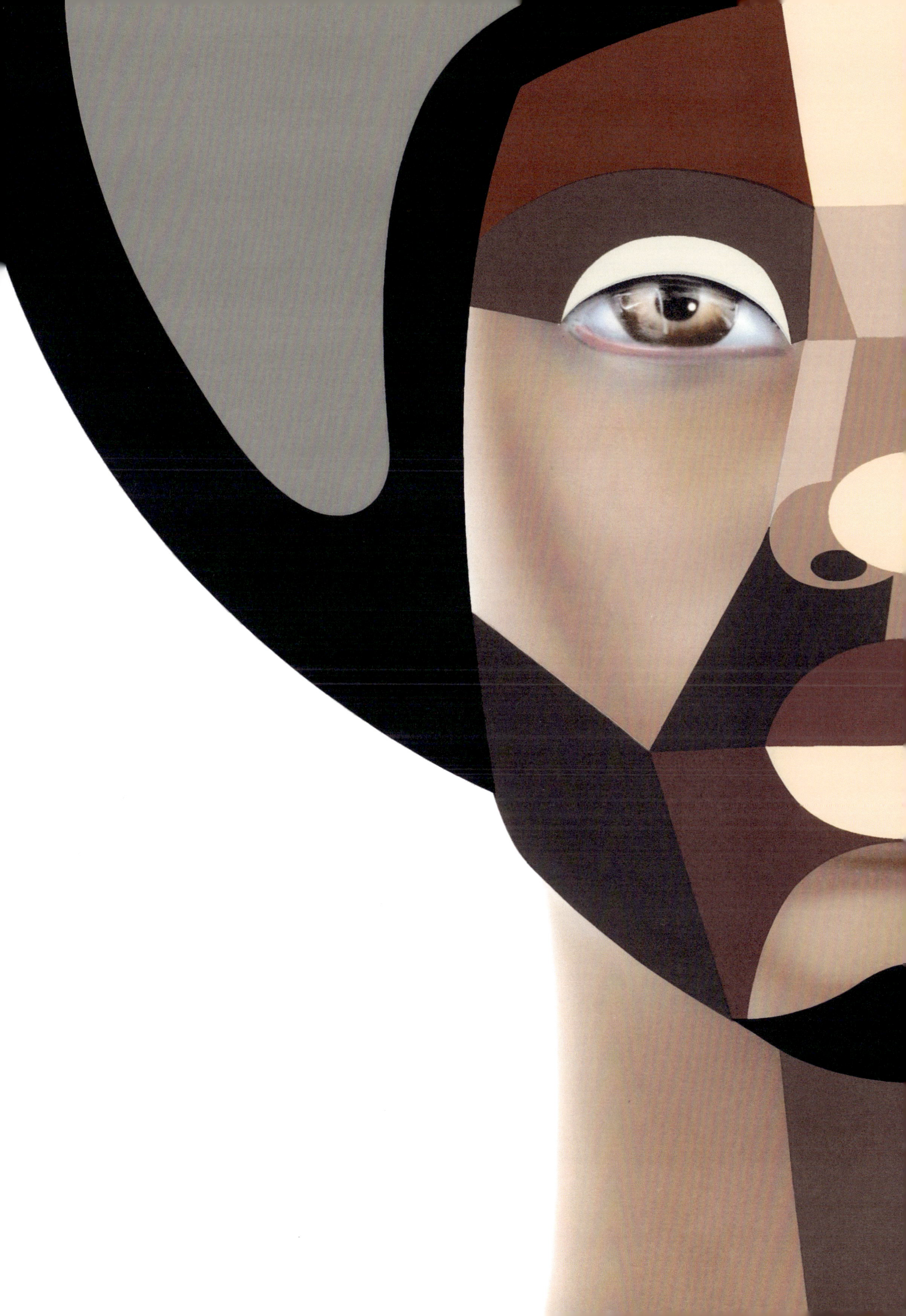

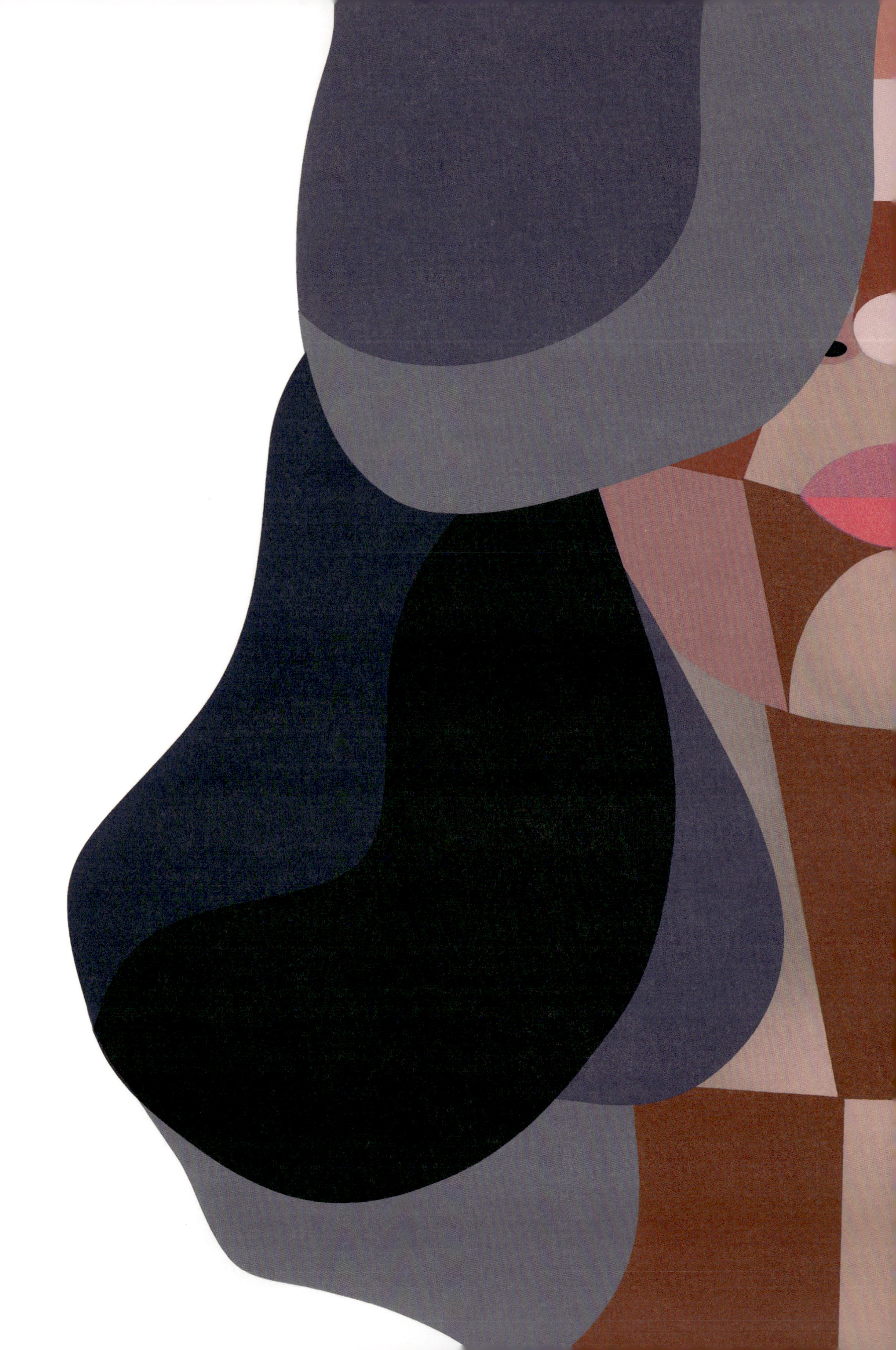

Style Variations
After Derrick Adams

by Krista Franklin

"Styles upon styles upon styles is what I have..."
—Phife Dawg

There's a million ways to fly.
On the wall of any beauty salon
barber shop lives an instructional
of cool. A manual, slides of side
views, fresh parts cut sidelong
along the cranium. Surgical precision.

Tucked in every town
is a sanctuary of style.
Suds scalps massaged and seated
beneath heated plastic dome
piece, ends clipped, snipped
smooth into glossy geometry.

Legend has it, okra traveled
the transatlantic tucked in the weft
woven against the head of some
loved one snatched from home.
Seeds nested next to hair follicles
seeded soil of a new nation.

And then there's the one
about freedom maps braided
into daughters' thick crowns,
aesthetic fugitivity, liberatory
cartography translated by fingers
deft and dangerous enough
to weave a plot in broad daylight.
The north star masquerades as cornrows.

Black hands touch tender
in rituals of adornment. Some
brother just stepped out
from behind his barber's
cutting cape looking super,
strutting out into open air.
Miss Lady's coiffed locks
turns heads like a carousel.
Every couple of weeks she sips
neighborhood tea spinning
slow in the salon shop seat.

There's a whole history
to this, practice of tiny touches,
this elaborate liturgy of beauty.

Previous: *Style Variation 1 (Afro)*, 2020 and *Style Variation 3 (Loose Wave)*, 2023 (detail)
Opposite: *Style Variation 2 (Waves)*, 2020 (detail)

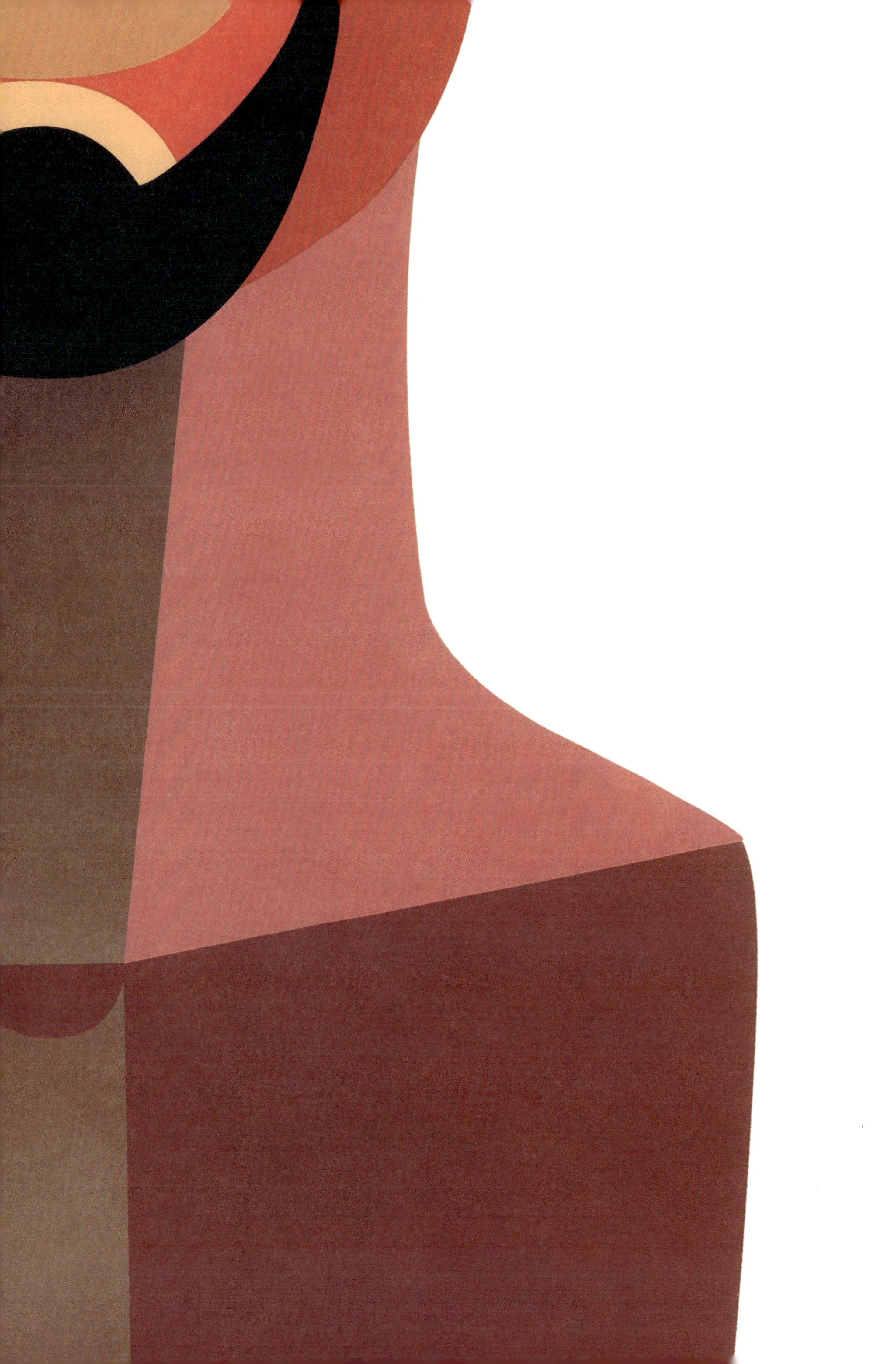

Style Variation 1 (Pixie), 2023
Screenprint and archival inkjet with acrylic gloss varnish on
Somerset Museum Rag Radiant White. Edition of 50. 27 × 20 inches.

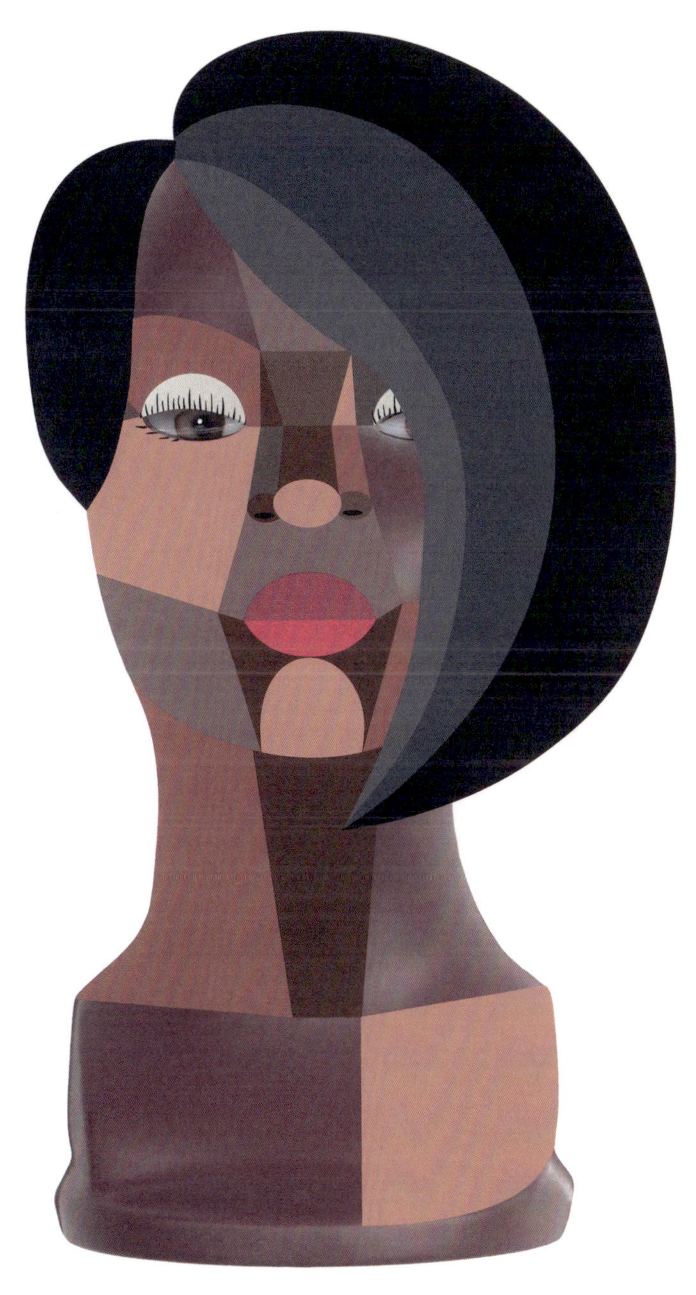

Style Variation 2 (Space Buns), 2023
Screenprint and archival inkjet with acrylic gloss varnish on Somerset Museum Rag Radiant White. Edition of 50. 27 × 20 inches.

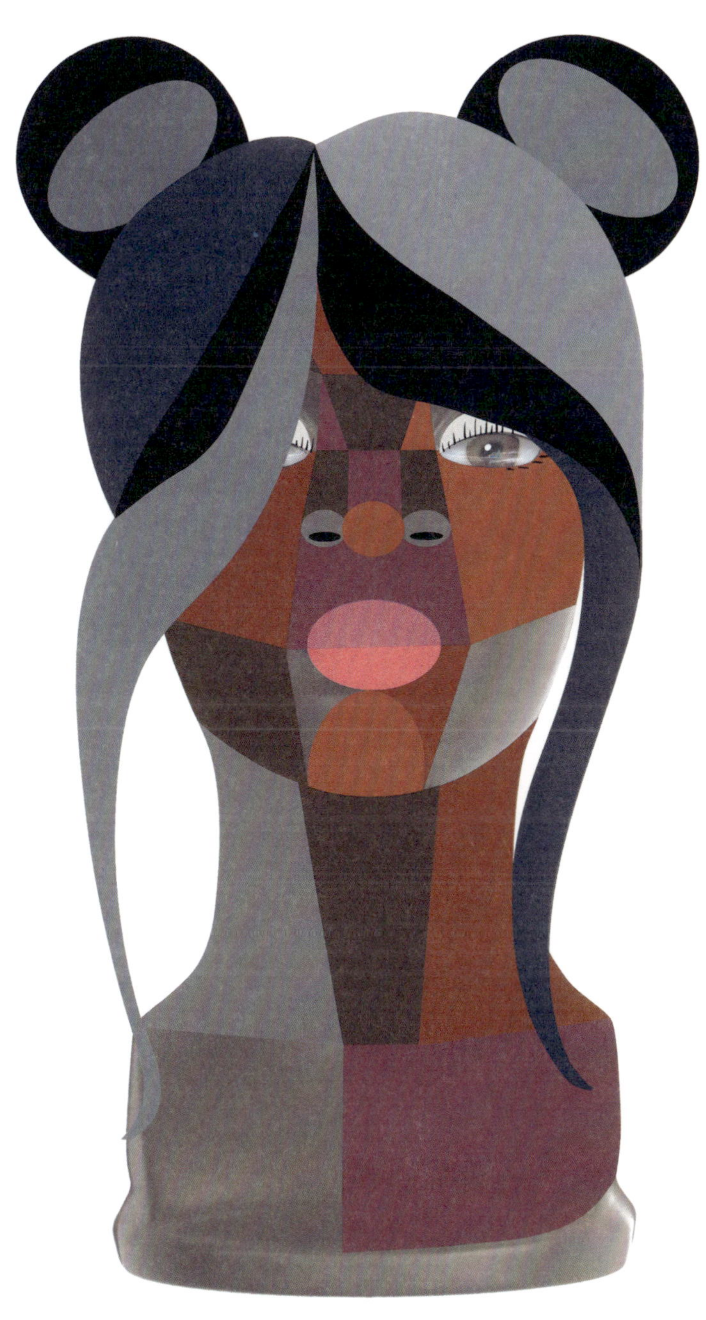

Style Variation 3 (Loose Wave), 2023
Screenprint and archival inkjet with acrylic gloss varnish on
Somerset Museum Rag Radiant White. Edition of 50. 27 × 20 inches.

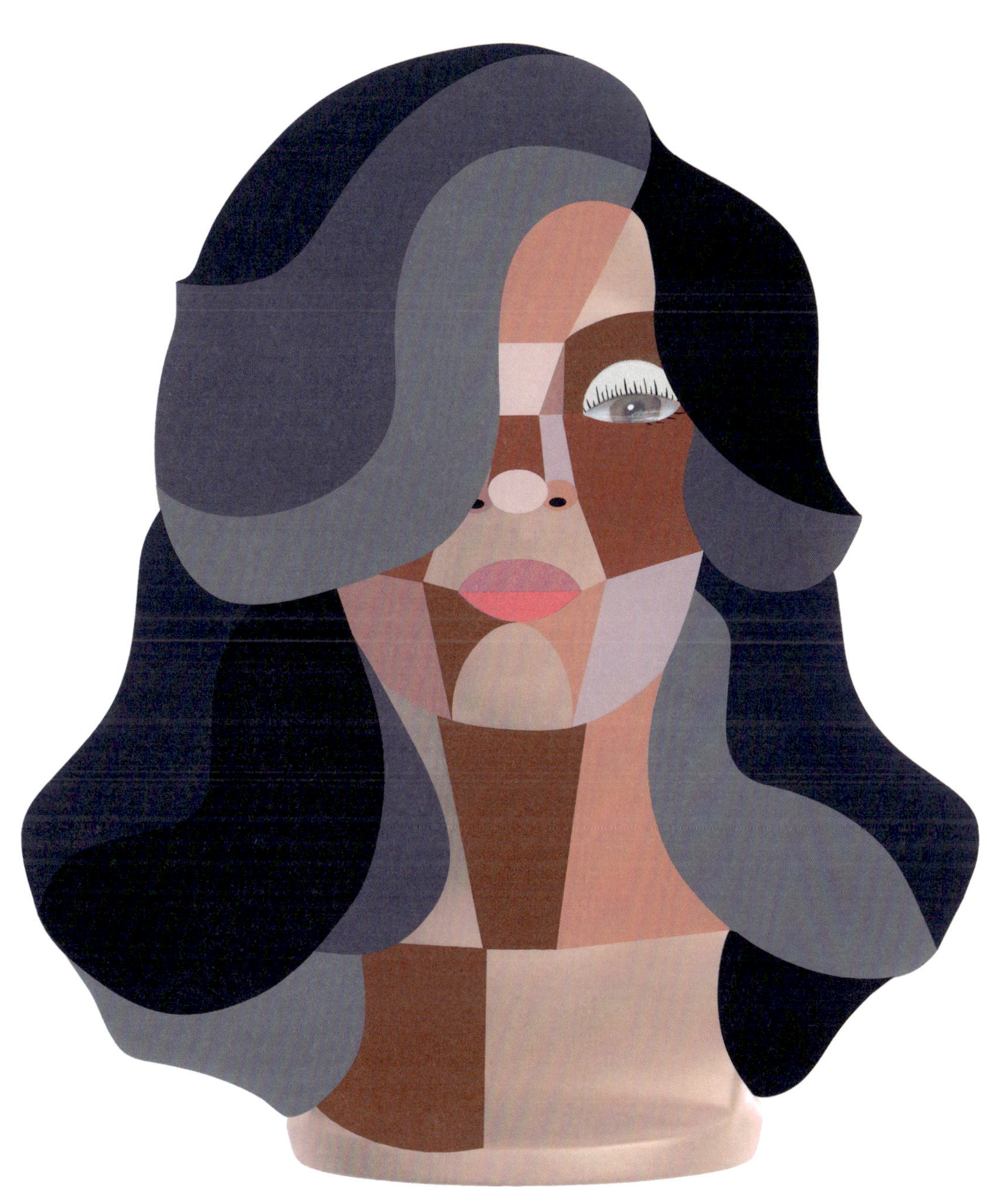

Style Variation 4 (Side Part), 2023
Screenprint and archival inkjet with acrylic gloss varnish on
Somerset Museum Rag Radiant White. Edition of 50. 27 × 20 inches.

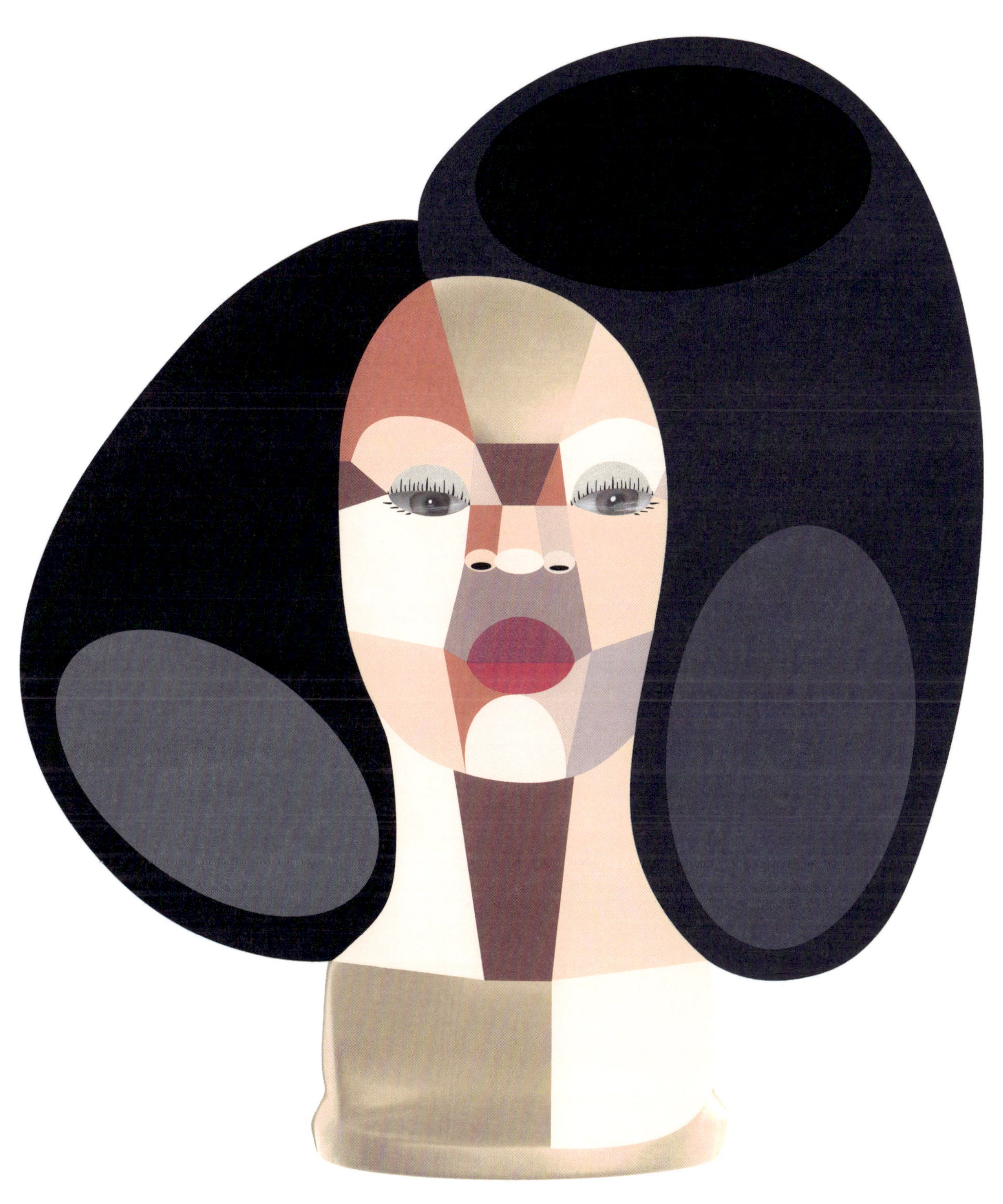

Style Variation 5 (Fringe), 2023
Screenprint and archival inkjet with acrylic gloss varnish on
Somerset Museum Rag Radiant White. Edition of 50. 27 × 20 inches.

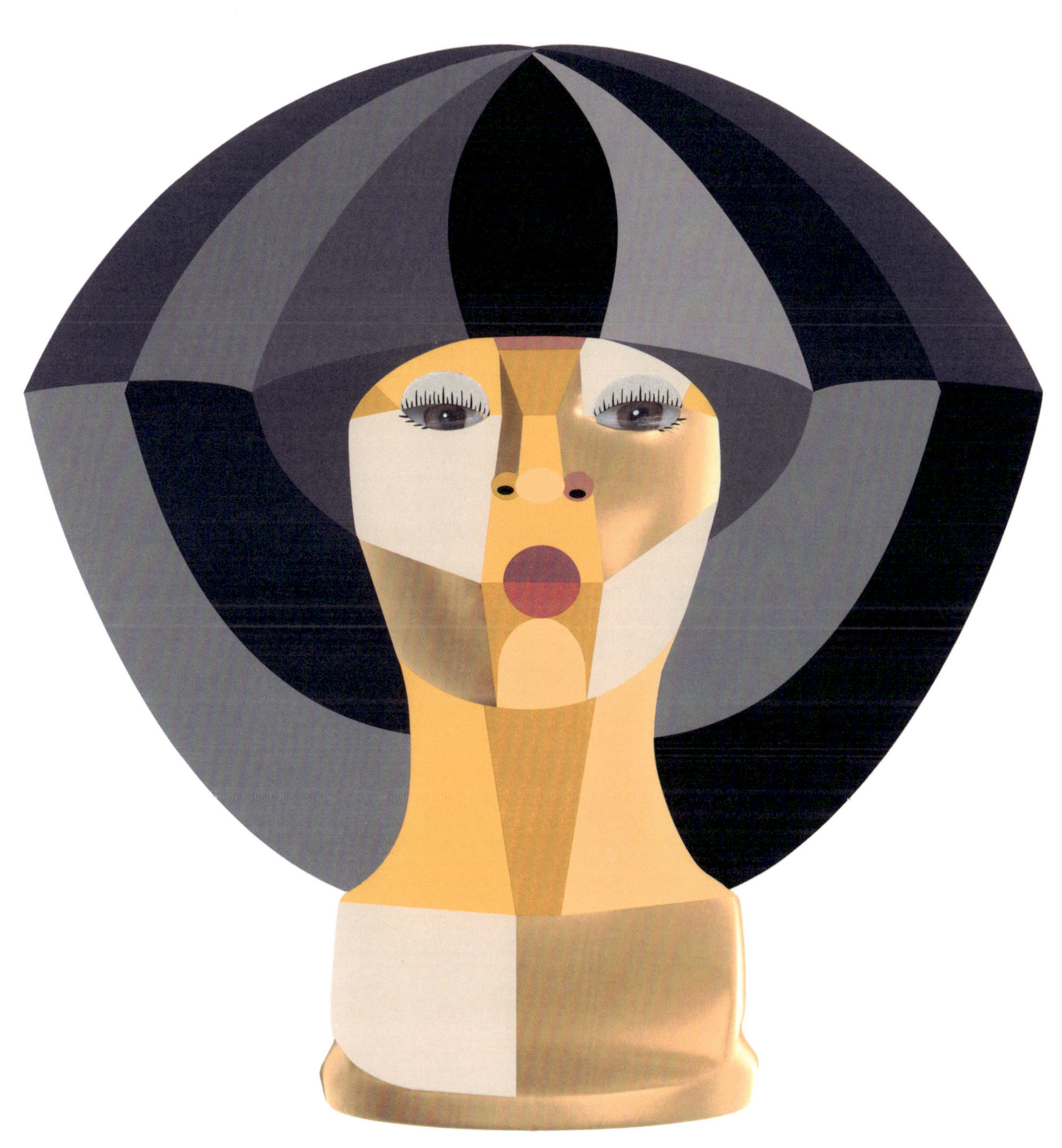

Style Variation 1 (Afro), 2020
Screenprint and archival inkjet with acrylic gloss varnish on
Somerset Museum Rag Radiant White. Edition of 30. 27 × 20 inches.

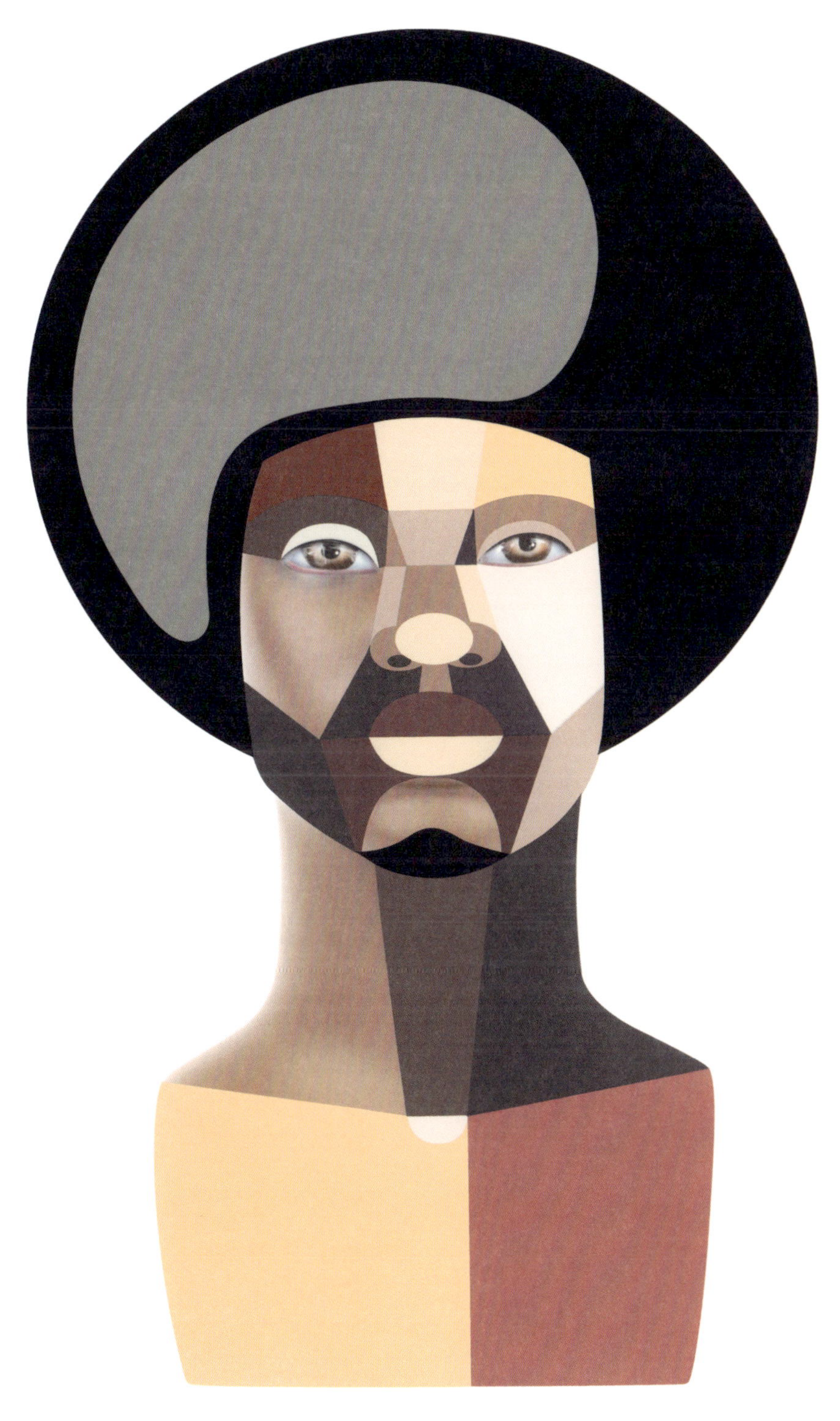

Style Variation 2 (Waves), 2020
Screenprint and archival inkjet with acrylic gloss varnish on
Somerset Museum Rag Radiant White. Edition of 30. 27 × 20 inches.

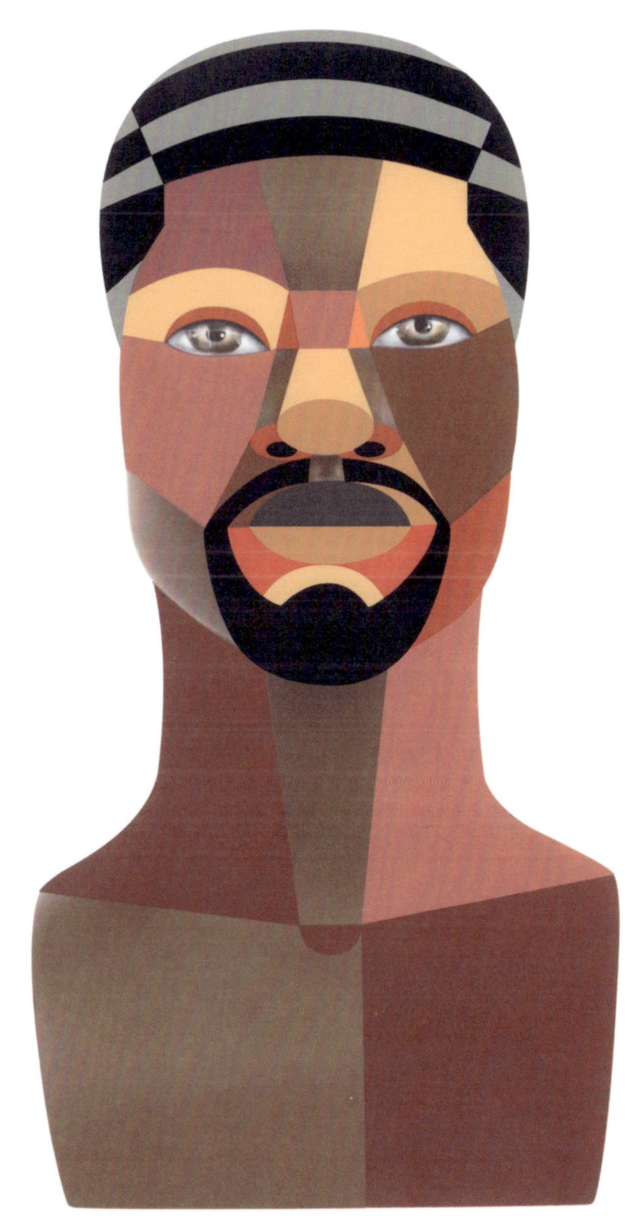

Style Variation 3 (High Top), 2020
Screenprint and archival inkjet with acrylic gloss varnish on
Somerset Museum Rag Radiant White. Edition of 30. 27 × 20 inches.

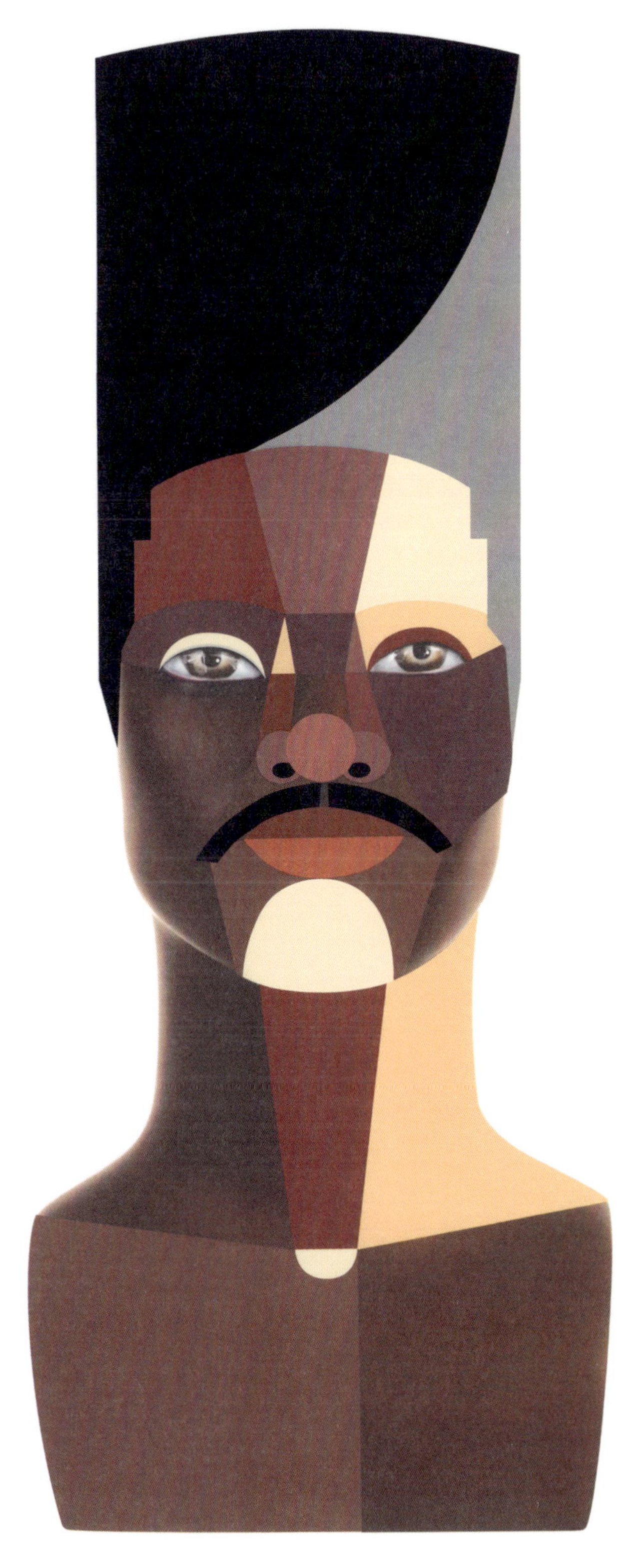

RTP

Style Variation 4 (Beard), 2020
Screenprint and archival inkjet with acrylic gloss varnish on Somerset Museum Rag Radiant White. Edition of 30. 27 × 20 inches.

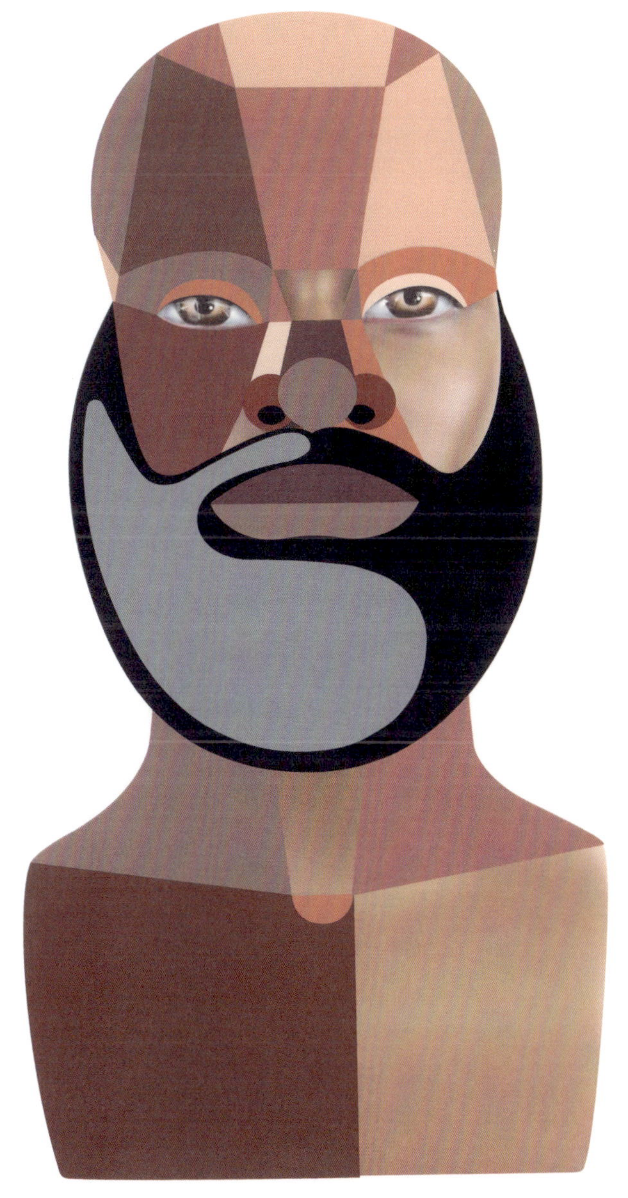

RTP

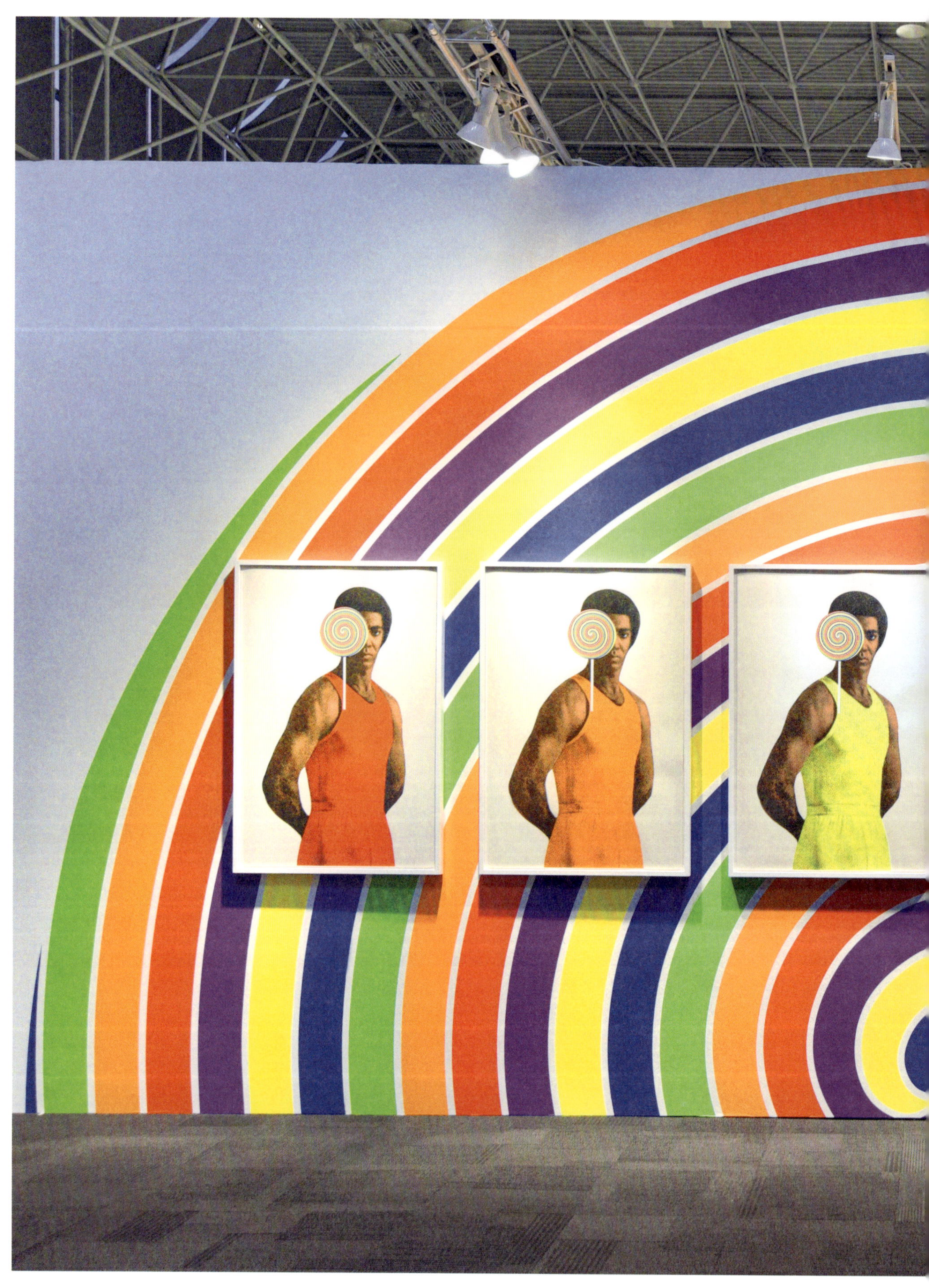

Eye Candy, 2023
Six-panel screenprint with relief and collage on Coventry Rag and Arches 88.
Edition of 24. Each panel 45 × 30 inches; Entire installation 12 × 24 feet.

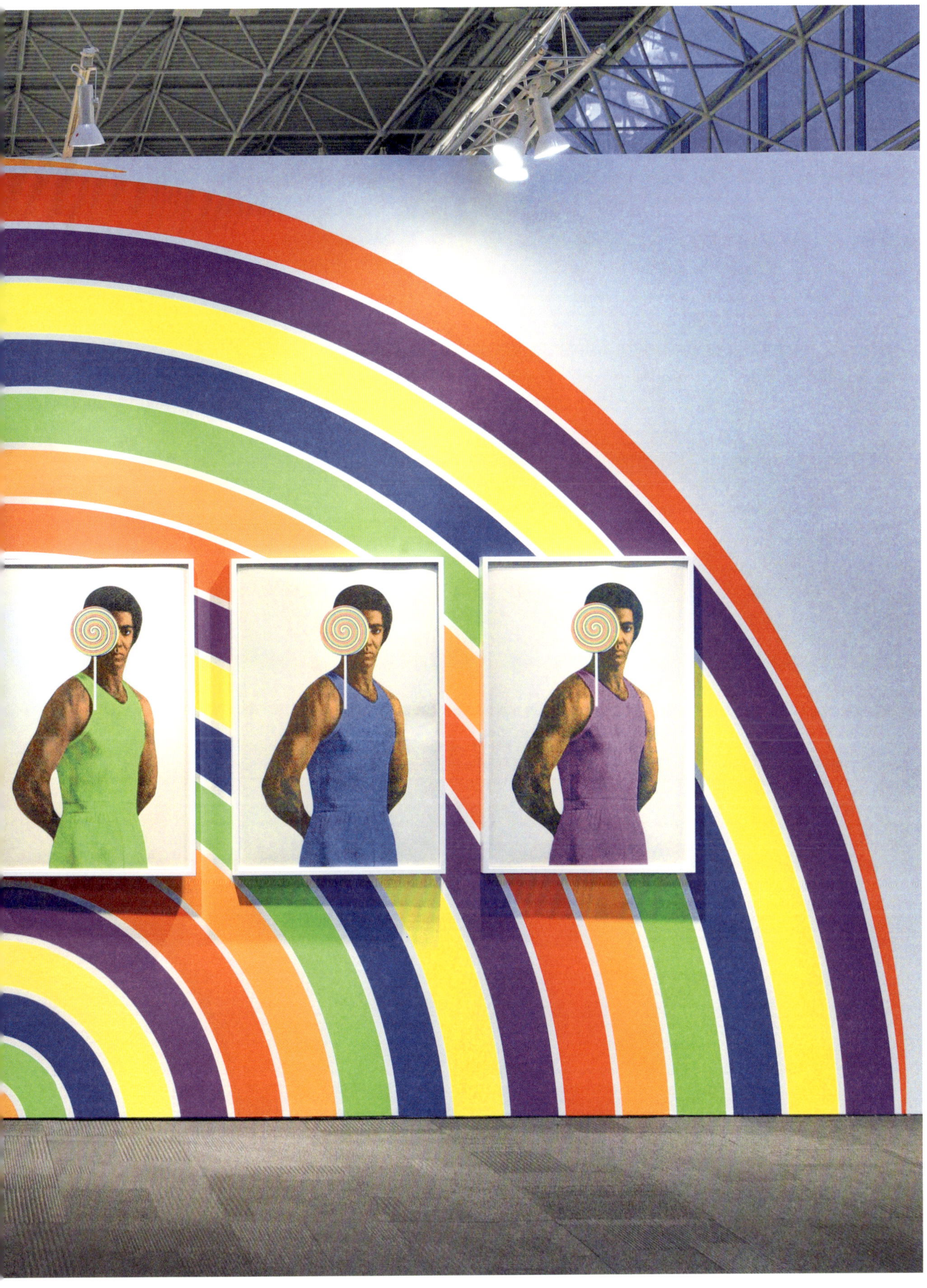

pp. 70–80: *Eye Candy*, 2023 (details)

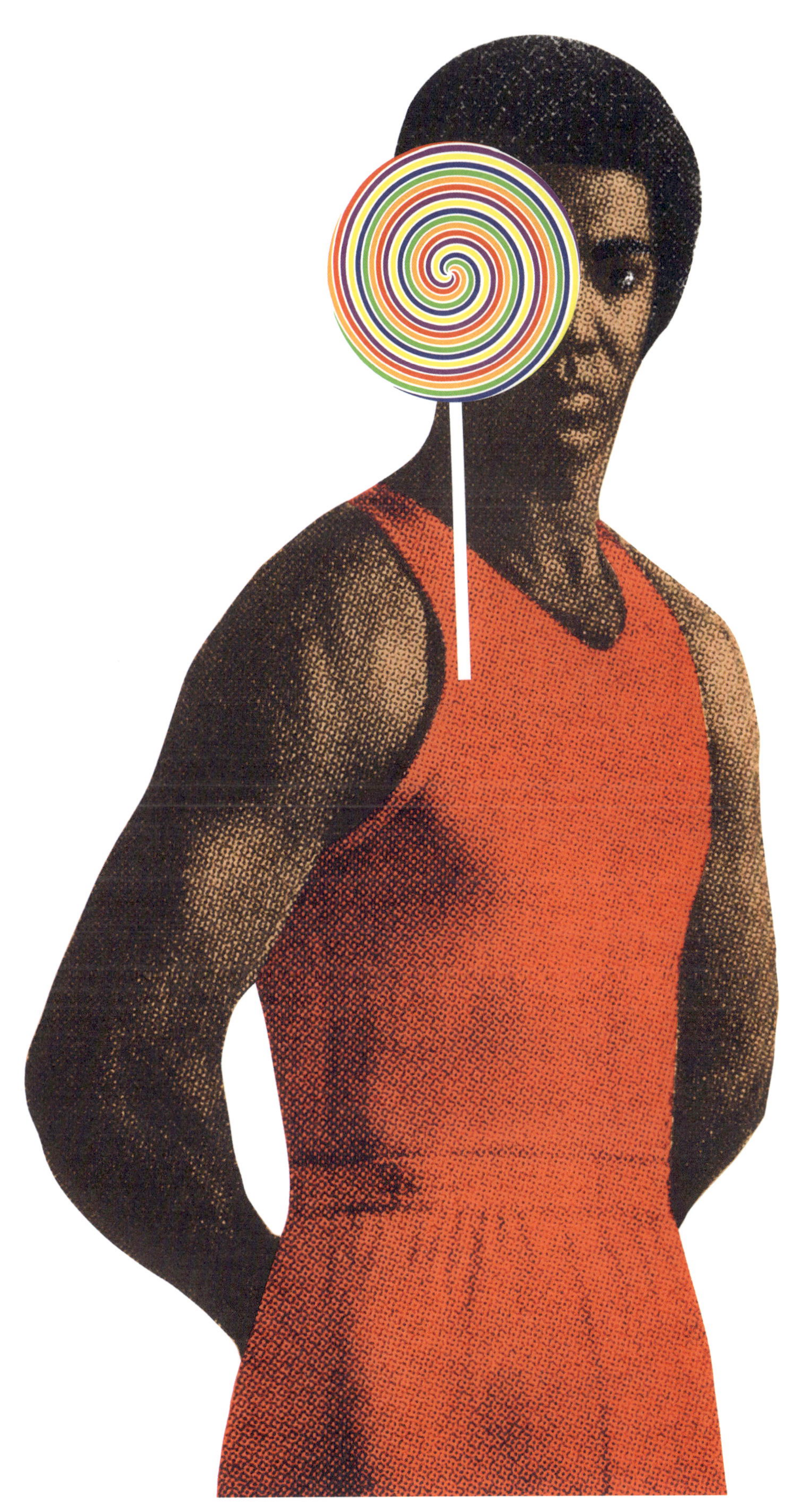

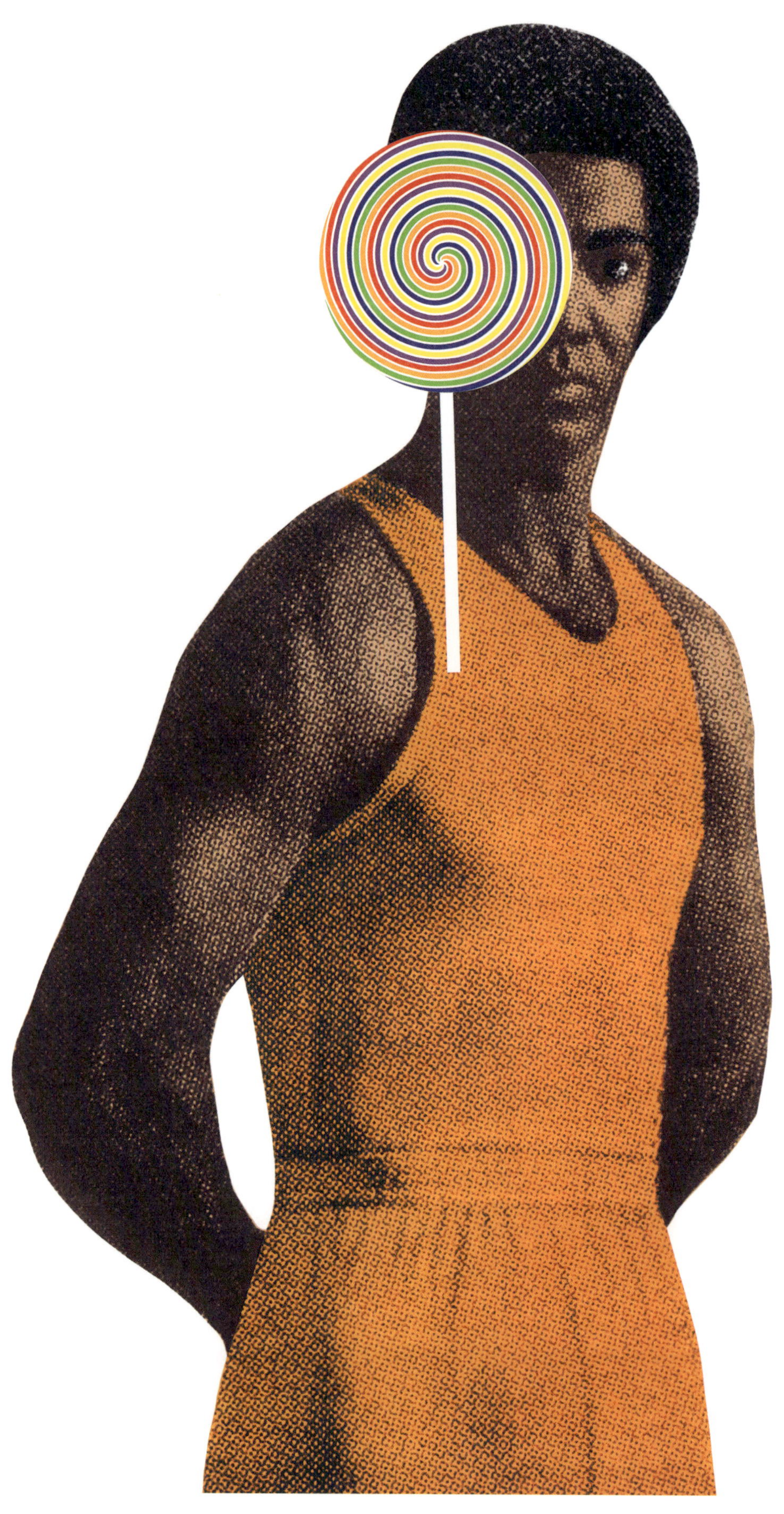

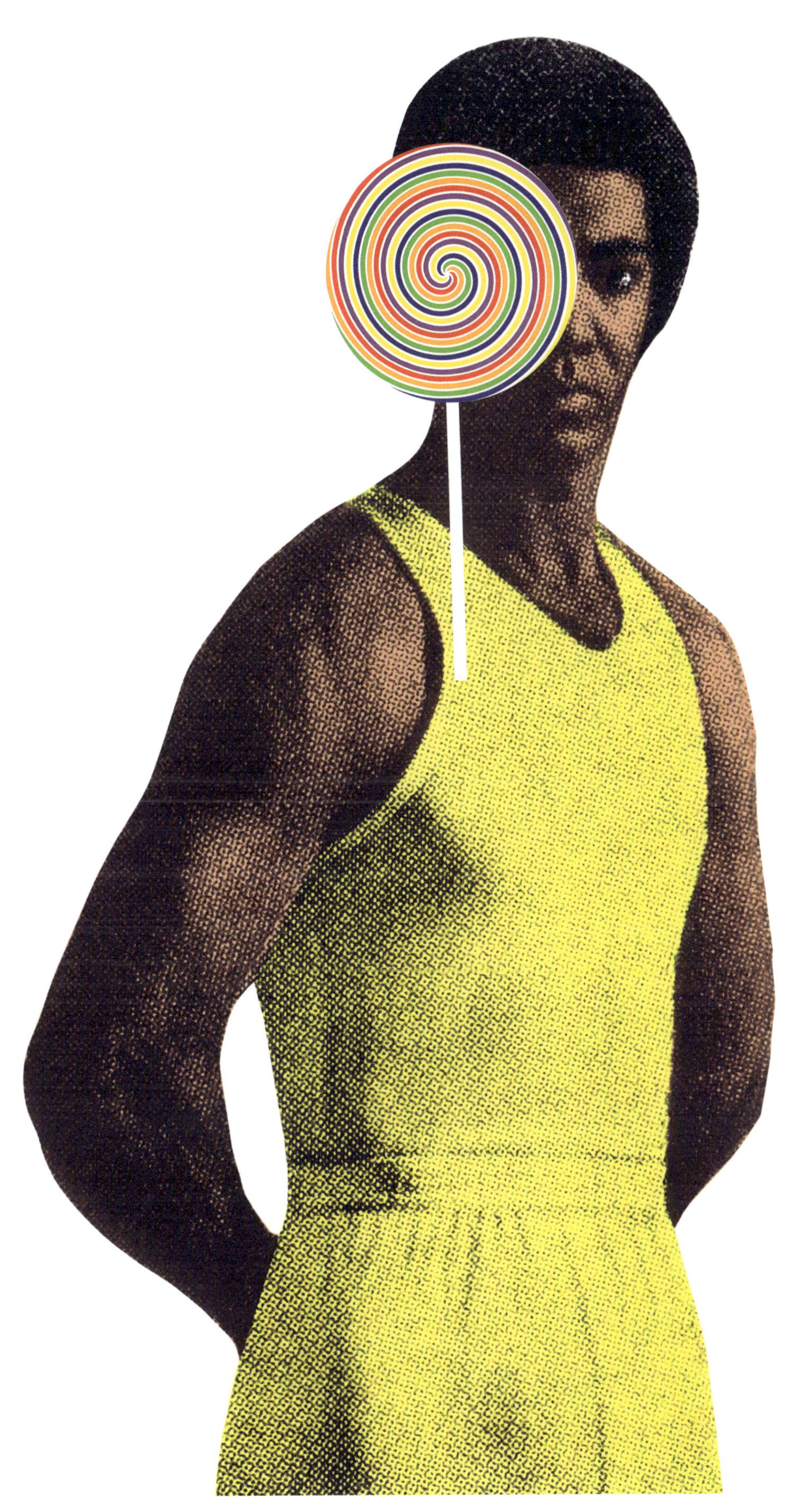

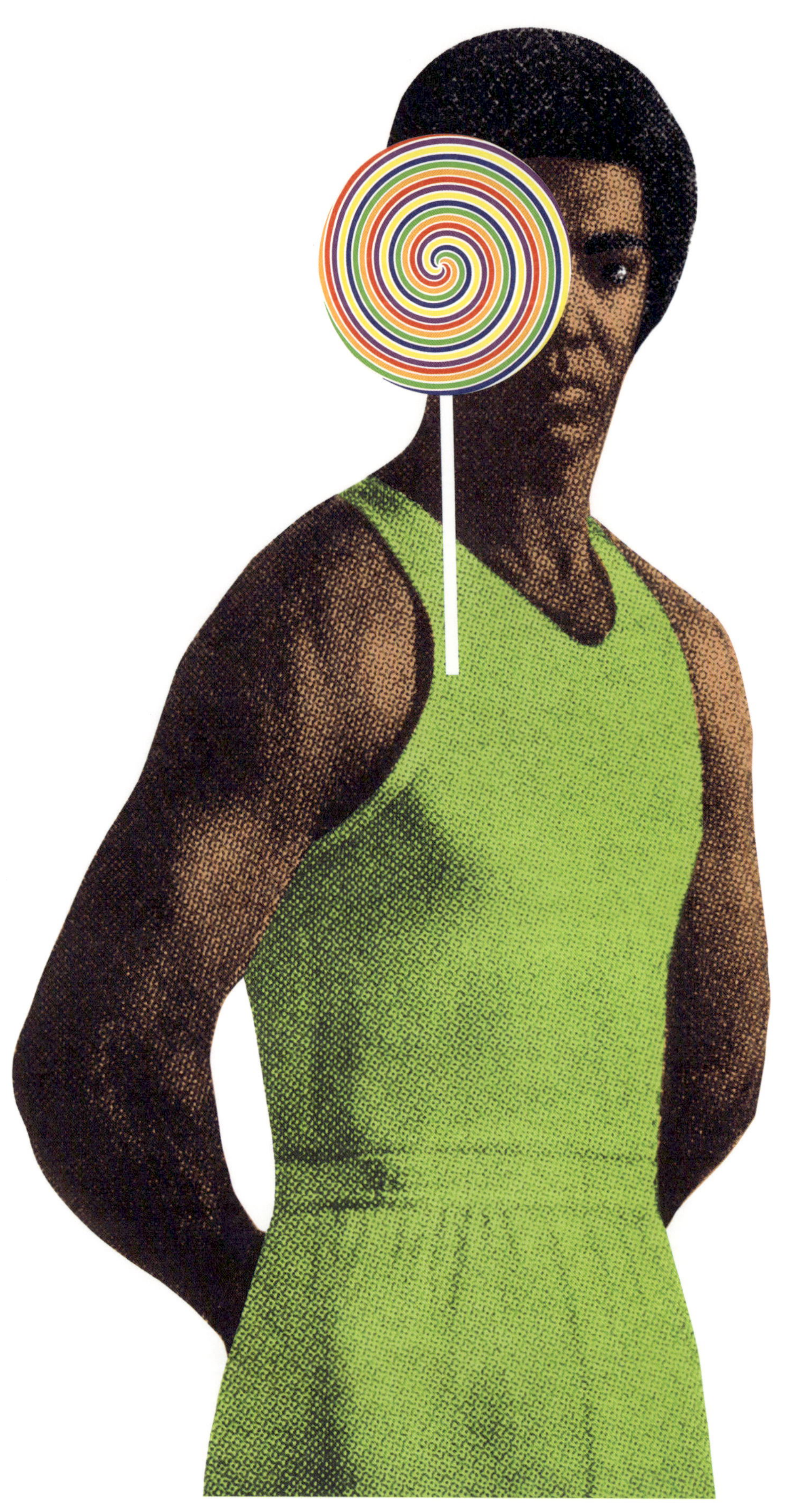

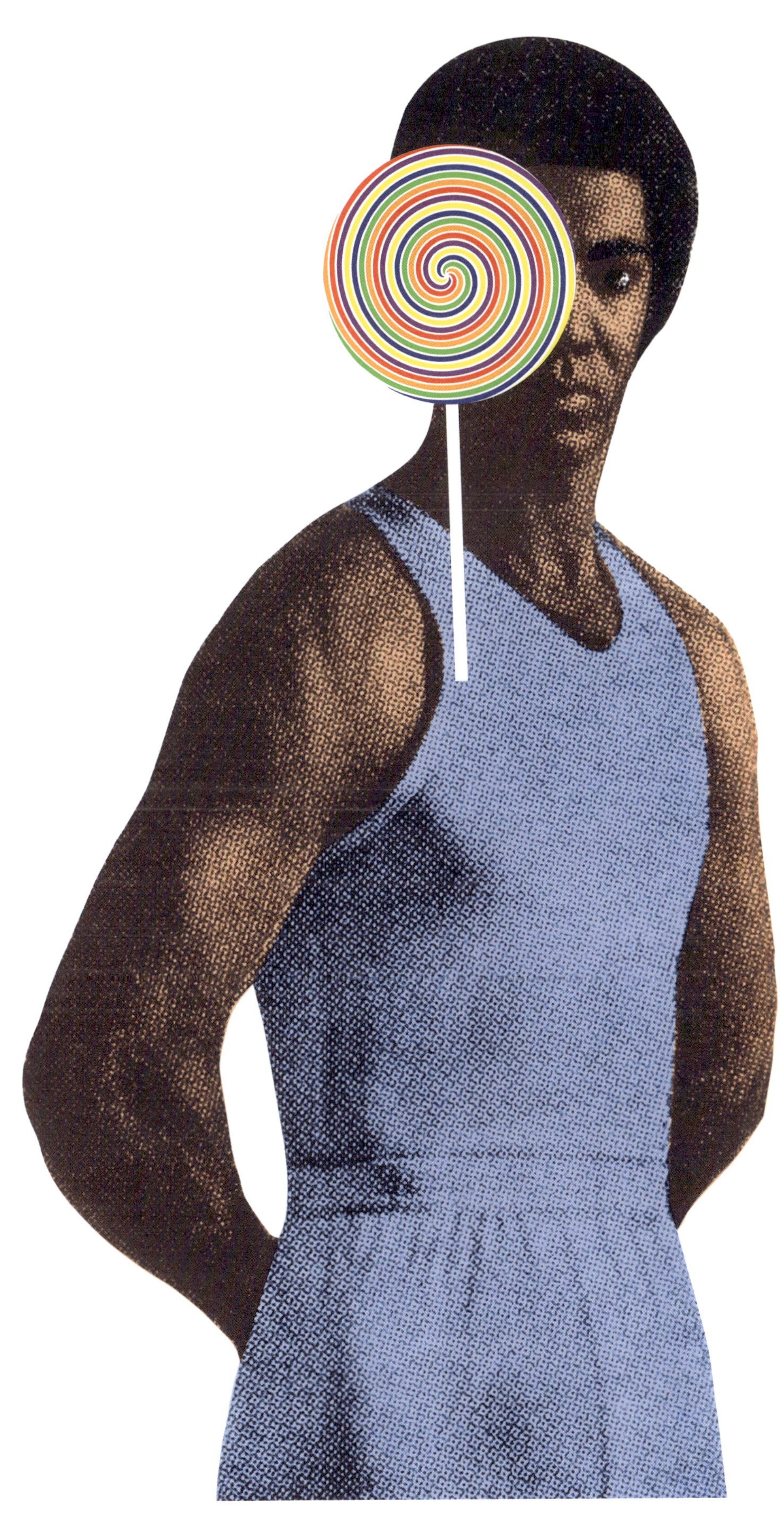

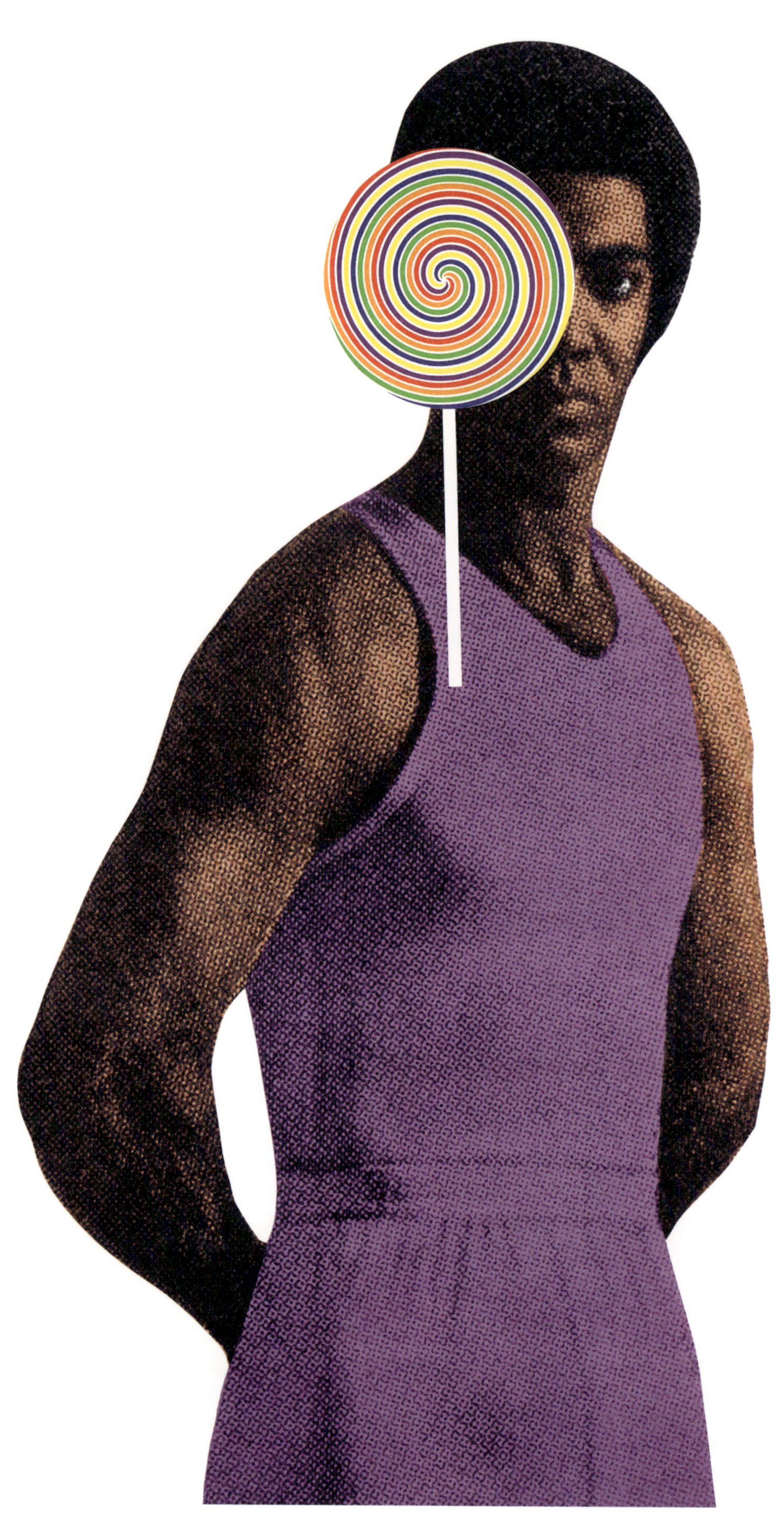

“It’s Not a Copy— It’s Its Own Thing”

An Interview with Derrick Adams

On October 10th, 2025, Derrick Adams sat down with Katie Geha, Director of Tandem Press, and Tandem Press's Collaborative Printmakers Joe Freye, Jason Ruhl, and Patrick Smyczek to discuss printmaking, experimentation, and collaboration.

KATIE GEHA

Derrick, can you talk about what brought you to Tandem? And to printmaking?

DERRICK ADAMS

I first became interested in prints when I was invited to Middlebury College to do a workshop with some students in printmaking through one of my college friends, Hedia Klein, who was heading the print department there. That was my first time actually working on a print in an educational setting, where the final piece would go into the Middlebury Museum's archive. It was also my first experience working with other people to produce something of mine, collaborating with a master printer and students to bring a print to life.

That experience really got me hooked. After that, Mickalene Thomas, who had just finished a project with Tandem, recommended me to Paula Panczenko, the director of Tandem at the time.

JASON RUHL

Right, so on that recommendation you came in 2019, and we began working on *Self Portrait on Float*. We used the laser engraver to cut the blocks, creating a six-block print [composed of] 94 pieces and 19 collaged elements. It was the first time we'd ever done something that complex. It was definitely the most ambitious puzzle-block print we'd made up to that point.

DERRICK

Yeah, it was a lot! I came in at the beginning just to mix colors, meet the team, and talk about format and scale. That first visit was all about experimenting, playing with material, adjusting color, and figuring out how the work would exist as a print.

JASON

We did *Self Portrait* and then *Boy on Swan Float*, and you were also talking about *Style Variations* around that time.

DERRICK

That's right. It just flowed from one project to the next.

PATRICK SMYCZEK
I think *Party Guest 1* was happening around that time, too, because I started working at Tandem in fall 2019. Joe and I visited your studio in Brooklyn, and you were working on the *We Came to Party and Plan* series.

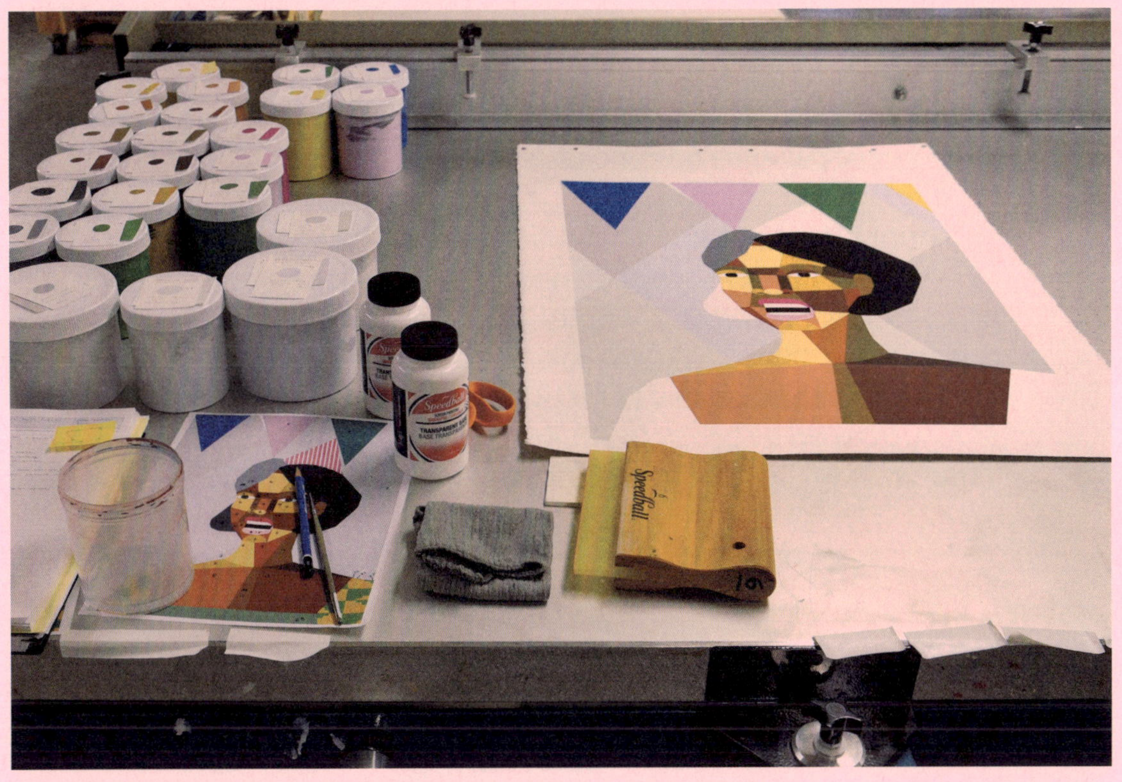

[1–2] *Party Guest 2* being editioned at Tandem Press, 2021.

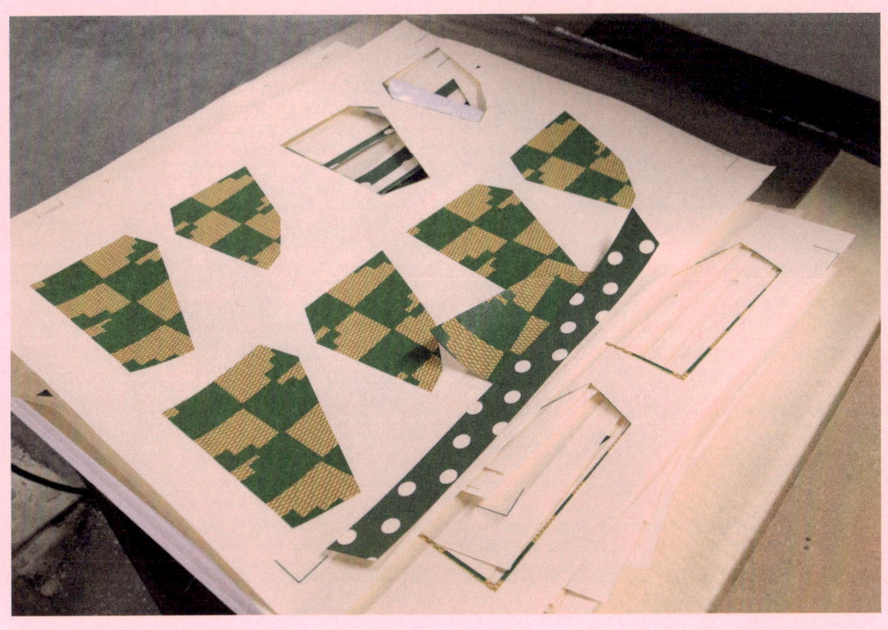

DERRICK

Oh yeah, exactly! Honestly, there really haven't been any breaks between projects. It flowed so seamlessly that, until yesterday, I hadn't realized how many prints we'd made. I didn't realize it was twenty, which I'm really excited about.

Printmaking has been a relief, in a lot of ways, from being in the studio working on unique works for other projects. It's a great way to think about accessibility and reaching a larger audience. It's also been beneficial because I could be in multiple exhibitions with the same print, which gave me more visibility for my practice beyond commercial galleries and museum projects.

The print world became an extension of my practice and my audience. I learned so much about collectors, the academic side, the process itself. It was this whole other world I tapped into through printmaking. It also gave me more space in my studio life: once a print was formed through experimenting and test printing, it freed me up to return to other projects while still checking in and collaborating at Tandem. It really started to feel like I had two studios.

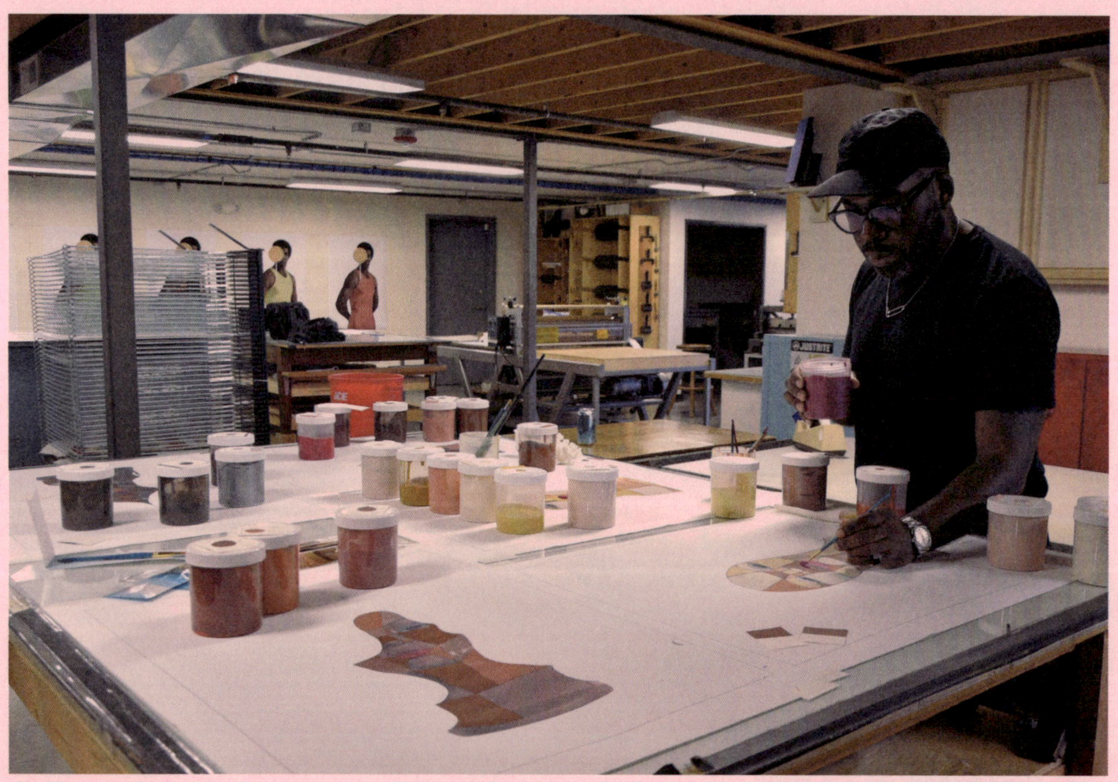

[3] Derrick Adams working in the Tandem Press studio, 2022.

That gave me a lot of mental space to know I could work one way in my studio and another way here, even in another city.

KATIE

What's it like collaborating on a print, versus working alone in the studio?

DERRICK

My relationship with the collaborative printers here at Tandem is really interesting. In my own studio, I use all sorts of materials without thinking about whether they can translate into a print. I'm focused on what I want to say and how I want to say it. Whether I'm working alone or with assistants, I'm focused on generating ideas that are challenging and exciting. That's the most mentally draining part: creating something that feels fresh. And that pressure multiplies when you're making an edition. That's what makes working with Tandem so great: the printers here are inclined to *encourage* difficult processes. They'll say, "Okay, how can we translate this three-dimensional thing you've made into something that *looks* three-dimensional through printmaking?" That kind of thinking has elevated my whole understanding of the medium.

I've worked with print shops where limitations dictated the outcome. Here, it's the opposite. The printers' experience allows them to offer ideas that elevate a print beyond what I'd initially envisioned, suggesting materials I didn't even know existed.

When I'm here, I want to make sure it's an image I won't get tired of seeing. That pressure, the idea of repetition, actually made me hesitant to start printmaking at first. But I've come to see it as one of the most generous art forms. It brings people into the process, both in production and collecting. It's a shared community.

KATIE

So, a question for the printers: how do you arrive at the process or technique when working with an artist?

JASON

The way we work now is pretty intuitive. We live with the image for a bit, think through ideas individually, and then come together to talk. For the *Party Guest* series, for instance, Patrick mentioned he'd worked with bookcloth before, so we decided to incorporate that into the clothing elements of the print. It helped us get closer to how Derrick approaches his work outside of the print studio.

The zippers in *Parlay* were a whole saga. I think it was just Patrick and me proofing those because Joe was out of town.

JOE FREYE

I was there when we started, but when I came back, they were totally different. I was shocked!

JASON

We had a week to get them proofed, framed, and sent off for the Armory Show. We were brainstorming how to handle the zippers, and I said, "We've got to figure out how to make these *not* actual zippers."

PATRICK

Yeah, the logistics would've been a nightmare in terms of storage, attachment, everything. So printing on paper made sense. Since we had used book cloth before, we knew how it behaved and decided to use that for the dice patterns. Each print really builds on the last; we take what we learned and use it in the next edition.

JASON

I always have Joe in my head saying, "I want to make a print," because that's what we do. So I went to JoAnn Fabrics, bought some zippers, scanned and manipulated them, and we printed from that. We sent it to you, Derrick, and it was the quickest you've ever responded.

DERRICK

I was blown away! The translation through print was so convincing. I needed it to *look* real. When I saw the test print, I knew it would be great. Every project we've done adds something new, some new material or idea that comes from experimentation and collaboration.

I like to throw in a little complication, just to see how you guys handle it. I think of you all as artists, and I don't want it to be boring. I like the challenge of doing something different each time. Even if it's a small change, it keeps me focused and engaged.

KATIE

How do you know when a work will translate well to print?

DERRICK

When I work on a series, I usually set one piece aside as the anchor. I keep it in my archive instead of selling it, and that's often the one I decide to edition as a print. But sometimes a work just comes out of the process here, like *Parlay*. Ideas often emerge directly from being in the studio with the printers, hanging out, experimenting. It can start in a lot of different ways.

KATIE
Printers, can you talk about how you work together? How are you able to get to an artist's visual language so quickly?

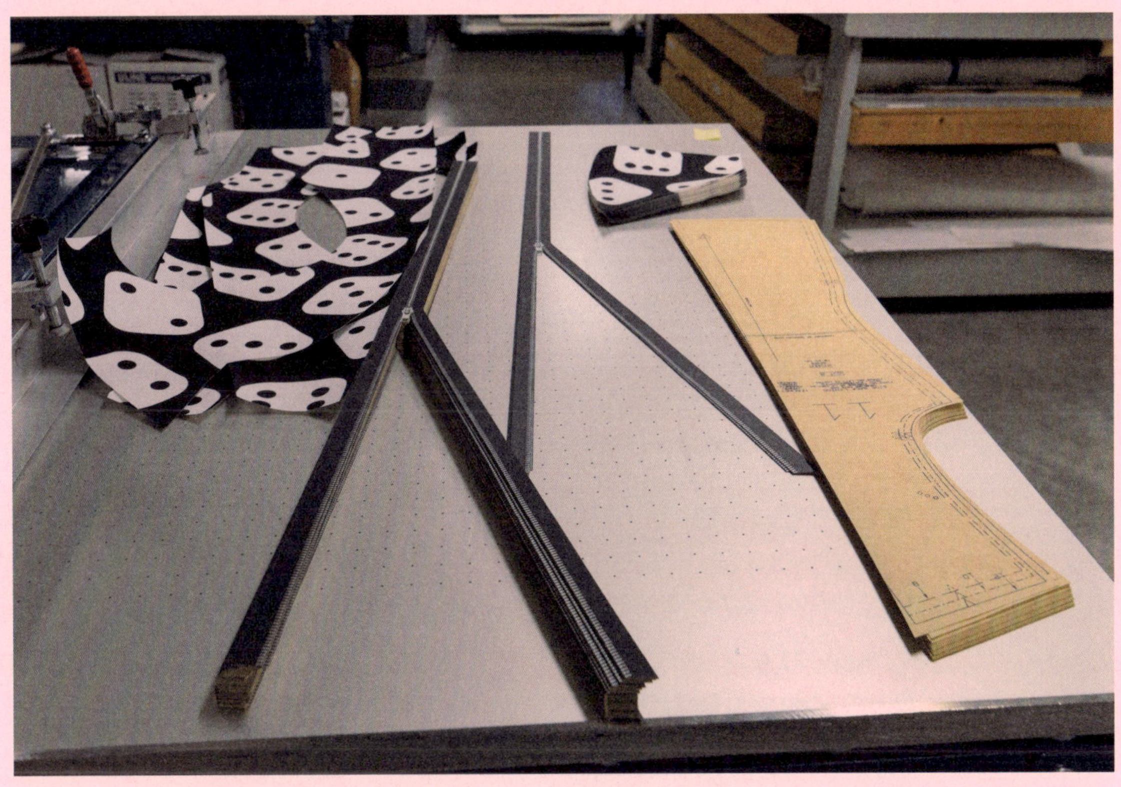

[4–5] *Parlay* being editioned at Tandem Press, 2023.

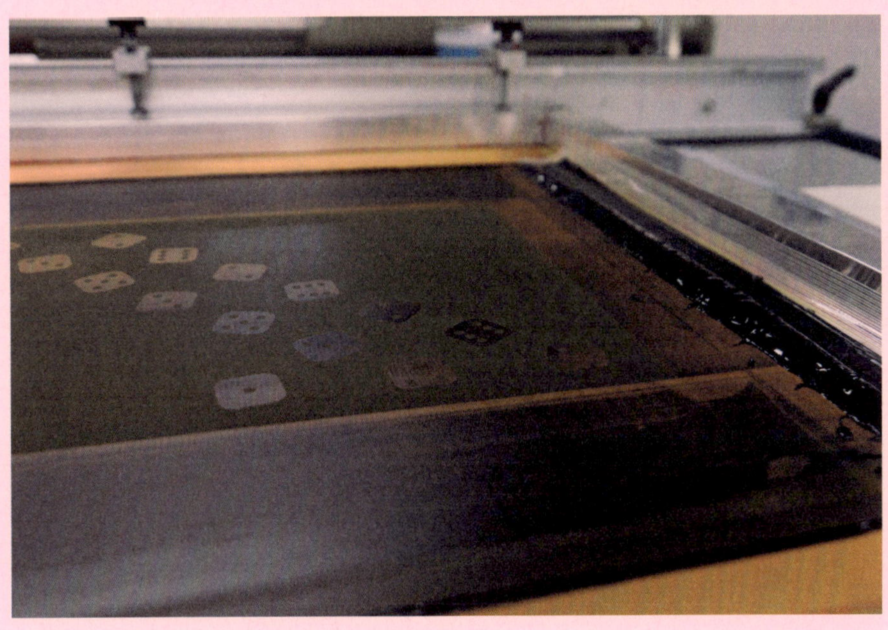

JOE

Honestly, I'm not sure. I think it's just years of experience and the fact that we each bring different skills to the table. Every time we start with a new artist, I get a little nervous wondering if it'll click, but it always does.

PATRICK

That's one of the best parts of the job. Working together on a new project means endless possibilities. Seeing something go from an idea to a finished print never gets old. We all bring our focus and experience to each project, and we care deeply about the artists, the work, and each other. We just want to make the best print possible every time.

JOE

Exactly. When we start a print, it's like a conversation that just takes off between the three of us and the artist. There's a level of confidence there, too. We work with artists we know we can truly collaborate with.

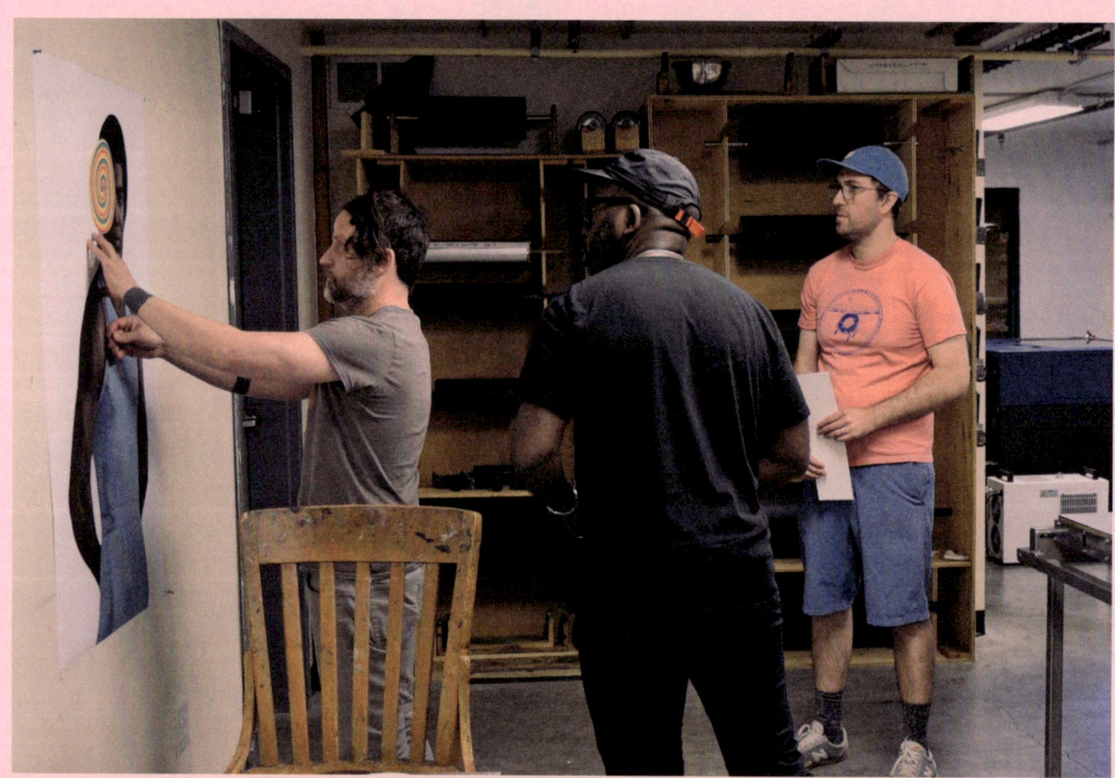

[6] Jason Ruhl, Derrick Adams, and Patrick Smyczek proofing *Eye Candy* at Tandem Press, 2022.

DERRICK

And that trust is everything. As an artist, when you're translating your work into print, trusting the people who are handling it is crucial. At this point, I come to Tandem sometimes just to say hi or have lunch. I know the print will turn out great. I feel completely confident in the process and the people.

KATIE

At Tandem, you often combine multiple processes in one print. How do you think about technology in relation to printmaking, an ancient technology itself?

JOE

I don't think about it. I'm rooted in the traditional side, but I'll go to Jason and say, "Can the computer do this?" and he makes it happen. I'm happy to push the limits, I just need him to work the machine.

PATRICK

We each have our strengths, and that's what makes it work. No one's stretched too thin trying to do something they're not familiar with, so we lean on one another's expertise.

JASON

I like to say we're like studio musicians. You come in with your part, I have mine, and we all get our solos. Things overlap, of course, and not every day in the studio goes smoothly. There's always at least one day during a visit that goes sideways but no one loses it.

PATRICK

Maybe two days, tops. But then it clicks. We have a limited window with the artist, so we find a rhythm fast. We take notes, work efficiently, and make sure we have what we need to move into production once they leave.

JASON

And when it comes to technology, we really have no limits. We can do any technique here. That freedom is exciting, for us and for the artist.

DERRICK

Which can be dangerous! I don't want any limitations on what's possible. Tandem isn't tied to one process, so I'll do something like adding zippers to *Parlay* without thinking about how that'll translate. I know Jason will be excited to figure it out.

JASON

[Laughs] That's generous. My first thought was, "What the hell are we going to do with this?" But that's why I love having the three of us. The pressure's shared. I really do feel like we can do anything—and every project reinforces that.

I wasn't trained traditionally as a printmaker, so I approach things differently. I don't start from process or technique. Instead I start with the question, *How do we translate this image*? That's what matters most.

JOE

When we did Derrick's first *Self Portrait on Float*, the original painting was very brushy and painterly. We weren't sure how he'd feel about the print being so graphic, but he didn't bat an eye.

JASON

Even though we printed the key block backwards on the first try.

DERRICK

[Laughs] Yeah, but that's the thing. Even when a print starts from an existing work, it becomes something new. It's not a copy, it's its own thing, a different translation. You have to be open to that.

That's what I love about prints: they live beyond the studio. A piece like *Self Portrait on Float* can be in three shows at once. [For] an artist, that's incredible.

I've also learned that there's a really strong print-collecting community, from individuals to major institutions, and I've come to understand it more through working with Tandem and their network of collectors. It's opened my eyes to so many new opportunities as an artist. I've met collectors who buy both prints and unique works, and they value the prints just as much as the paintings.

For my generation of artists, there's sometimes hesitation around making prints, maybe a feeling that seeing an image more than once diminishes its uniqueness. But I've realized how high the level of commitment and connoisseurship is among print collectors. It's an honor to be in collections alongside artists I've long admired, people whose work these collectors have been following for decades.

I'm constantly learning how vital and relevant printmaking is in the contemporary art world. And because of that, I always want the quality of my prints to match the quality of my studio work. That's something I've consistently found in my collaborations with Tandem.

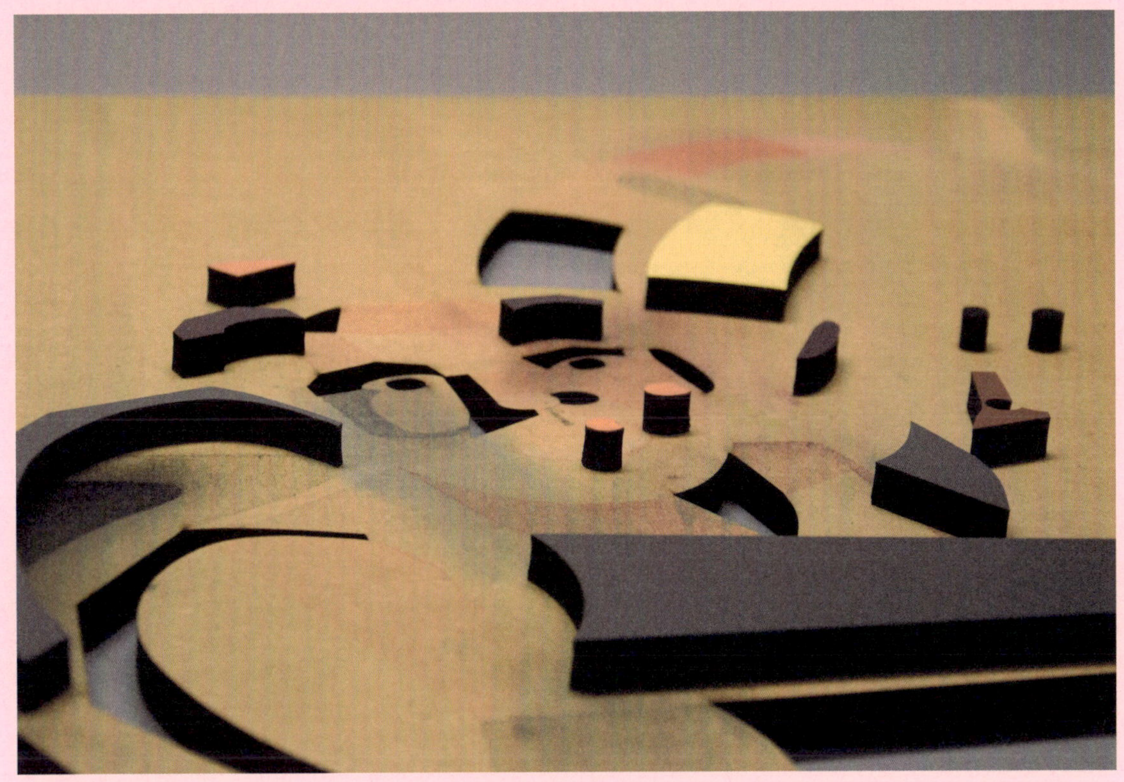

[7–8] Jason Ruhl and Joe Freye proofing *Self Portrait on Float* at Tandem Press, 2019.

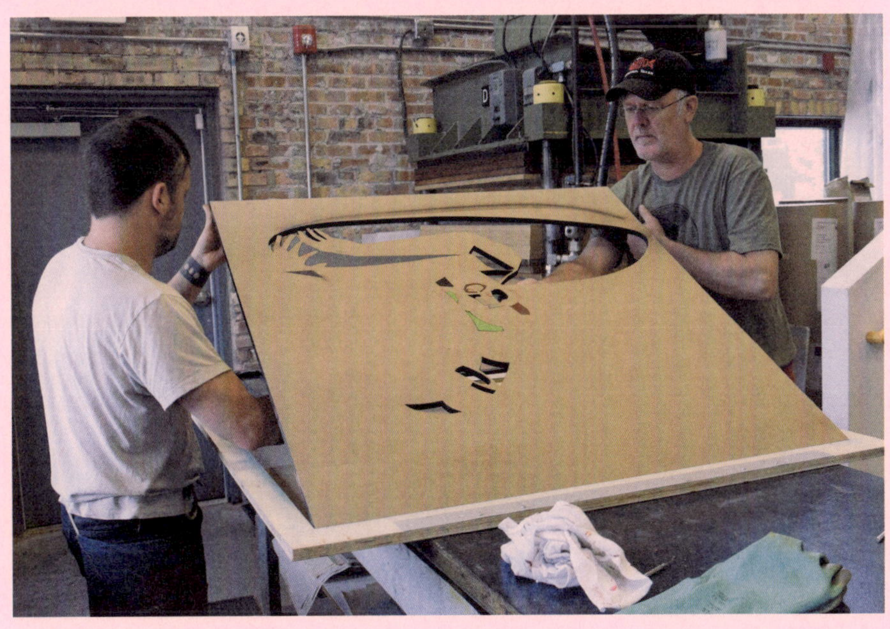

KATIE
I wondered if we could reflect on your first print made in 2019, *Self Portrait on Float*, in comparison to your most recent one made in 2024, *Where My Girls At?*

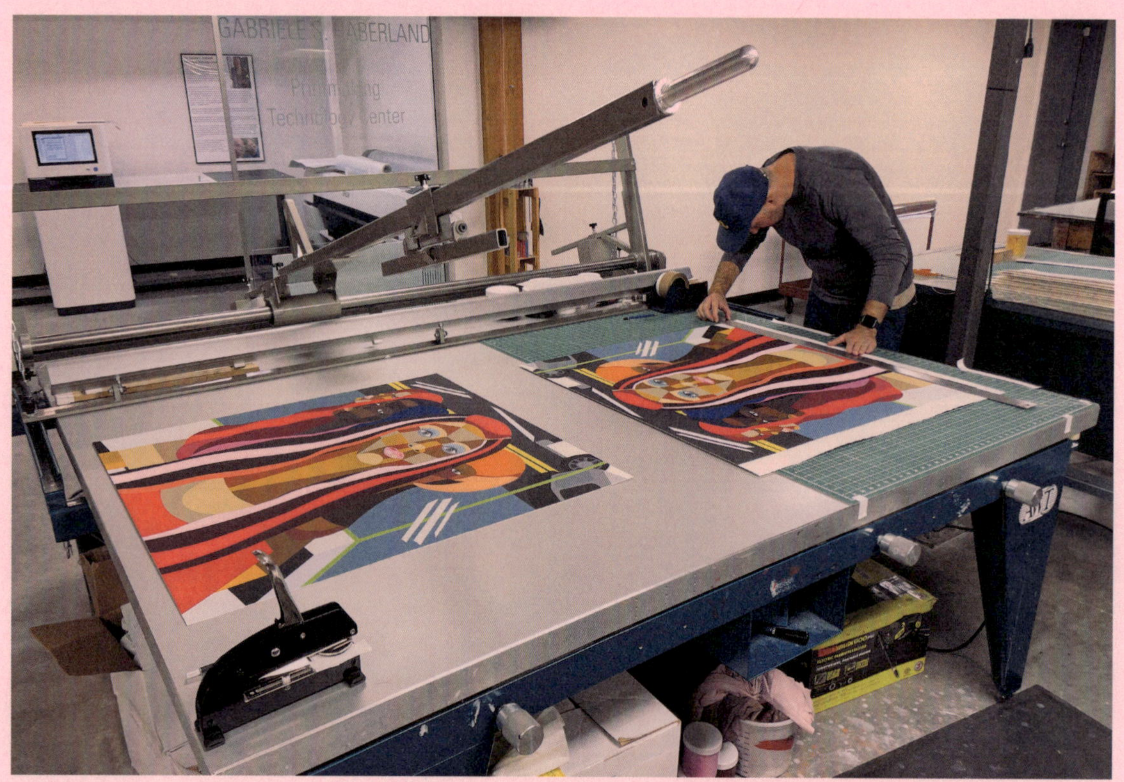

[8–9] Patrick Smyczek editioning *Where My Girls At?* in the Tandem Press studio, 2024.

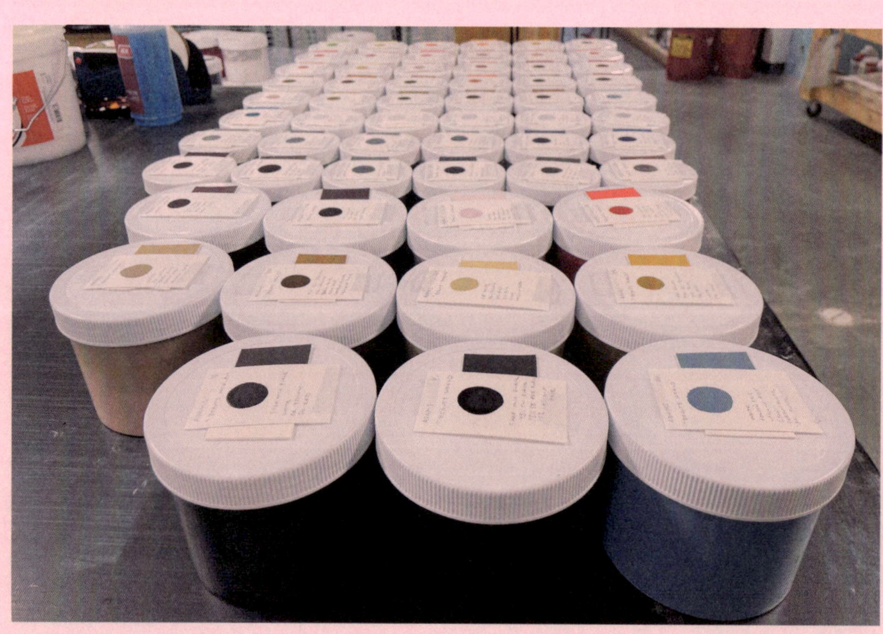

DERRICK

Well, *Self Portrait on Float* had a lot of color, but *Where My Girls At?* took it to a whole other level. When I decided to make it into a print, I was excited but also a little nervous because it had *so many* colors. The original painting is about half the size of the print, and I knew it needed to be bigger. Sometimes when I finish a smaller painting, I realize it should've been larger, and this was one of those cases.

Working with Tandem, I knew it would be a challenge, especially translating the metallics from paint to printmaking ink, which behaves so differently. But that's what made it exciting. The original painting hangs in my house, but the print gives people a chance to experience the work at the scale and energy I always imagined.

PATRICK

When you work with an artist over many years, you start to really understand how they think about color and composition. *Where My Girls At?* was complex. There are so many colors, each printed separately, all needing to line up perfectly. A tiny shift and the whole print could fall apart. But because we've worked with Derrick so much, the process felt natural. We knew it would be beautiful.

DERRICK

Yeah, there's a real shorthand now. Even though I use bright colors, there's always this earthy undertone, and the team understands that balance, how my colors work in terms of temperature and tone. It's amazing to see how much we've done together over the years.

Contributors

Derrick Adams is a multidisciplinary artist living and working in Brooklyn, New York. Adams's work celebrates and expands the dialogue around contemporary Black life and culture through scenes of normalcy and perseverance. He received his BFA from Pratt Institute and an MFA from Columbia University. In addition to his critically acclaimed art practice, Adams is a tenured associate professor in the School of Visual, Media and Performing Arts at CUNY Brooklyn College. He holds an honorary doctorate from Maryland Institute College of Art and established Charm City Cultural Cultivation, a non-profit organization to support and encourage underserved communities in his hometown of Baltimore.

Adams has mounted several notable public installations and has been the subject of numerous solo exhibitions at galleries and institutions worldwide. His art resides in the collections of the Brooklyn Museum, The Metropolitan Museum of Art; Studio Museum in Harlem; Whitney Museum of American Art; Virginia Museum of Fine Arts; and Birmingham Museum of Art, among many others. His highly anticipated first monograph was recently published by Phaidon/Monacelli, and in April, 2026, Adams will open, *View Master*, his first mid-career survey at the Institute of Contemporary Art, Boston.

Krista Franklin is a writer, performer, and visual artist, the author of *Solo(s)* (University of Chicago Press, 2022), *Too Much Midnight* (Haymarket Books, 2020), the artist book *Under the Knife* (Candor Arts, 2018), and the chapbook *Study of Love & Black Body* (Willow Books, 2012). She is a Cave Canem fellow, a Helen and Tim Meier Foundation for the Arts Achievement Award, and the Joan Mitchell Foundation Painters and Sculptors Grant recipient. Her visual art has exhibited internationally, and appeared as set dressing for music videos and national television programs.

Judy Hecker is Executive Director of Print Center New York, the nonprofit organization that champions printmaking as an art form that drives invention, collaboration, and access, and plays a vital role in society. In addition to her leadership role there, Hecker has organized exhibitions including the collaborative *Reprint* (2024) and co-curated *Nicole Eisenman: Prince* (2023; with Jenn Bratovich). Prior to the Center, Hecker was Assistant Curator in the Department of Drawings and Prints at The Museum of Modern Art, New York, where she contributed to exhibitions, acquisitions, and public programming. She co-curated MoMA's presentation of *William Kentridge: Five Themes* (2010; originally SFMOMA) and curated *Impressions from South Africa: 1965 to Now: Prints from The Museum of Modern Art* (2011). Other exhibitions curated include *Repicturing the Past/Picturing the Present* (2007); *Since 2000: Printmaking Now* (2006); *One Thing After Another* (2000); and *Ensor/Posada* (1999; co-curated with John Elderfield). Hecker earned her BA from Wellesley College and her MA from the University of Chicago.

Acknowledgements

Thank you to the generous donors who made this project possible: Linda DiRaimondo and Patrick Crean, Jay and Kim Handy, Kate Heaney, Chele Isaac and John Neis, Margaret LeMay, Paula and Russell Panczenko, John Wiley and Tess Arenas, and Mary Alice Wimmer. Enormous gratitude goes to Michael Gerdes for his deeply impactful support of this publication. I am in awe of the indefatigable Tandem staff—thank you, Joe Freye, Rachael Griffin, Seth Klekamp, J Myszka Lewis, Sona Pastel-Daneshgar, Jason Ruhl, and Patrick Smyczek. Adam Squires showed patience and good humor throughout the design process of this beautiful book, and I am grateful for his collaborative spirit. Judy Hecker and Krista Franklin bring insight and elegance to their interpretations of Adams's work, and I am deeply appreciative of their thoughtful prose. Thank you to Alyssa Alexander for keeping this project running smoothly and for responding to countless emails and questions with such speed and grace. Finally, I am profoundly grateful to Derrick Adams—thank you for trusting Tandem with your vision and for your unwavering generosity and friendship.

This publication was made possible from a grant by the Anonymous Fund and the Brittingham Wisconsin Trust.

ISBN
979-8-218-82400-6

Editor
Merray Gerges

Photography
Seth Klekamp
Sona Pastel-Daneshgar

Design
Adam Squires, assisted by
Jasmine Kan, CHIPS

Printed in the Netherlands
by Wilco Art Books

(Front cover)
Derrick Adams
Where My Girls At?, 2024 (detail)
Screenprint
36 × 36 inches.